THIS TIME
IT'S ABOUT

A 60-DAY JOURNEY

TO DISCOVERING

THE REAL ME

THIS TIME
IT'S ABOUT
Me

A 60-DAY JOURNEY

TO DISCOVERING

THE REAL ME

Ruth Langhorn and Michelle S. Lazurek

DEDICATION

To you, woman,

Explore and discover the real you

ACKNOWLEDGMENTS

Writing a devotional book was harder than I thought but more rewarding than I ever dreamed. None of this would be possible without several people who helped along the way.

Ruth would like to thank:
My husband and best friend Marcel, who always believed in me. Thank you boo bee cakes for all you do.
I'm eternally grateful to Michelle who helped me to birth this book. She was an excellent midwife and helped this dream become a reality.
To my daughter Deena, my brilliant Personal Assistant. I love you baby girl.
To Apostle Torrey who prophesied this book to come over my life. Thank you for being a light.
To Selina, my sister who saw in me what I could not see. Thank you for believing in me. Your next sis!
A very special thank you to my entire D3 Tribe who prayed for me throughout the process. D3! Yaye Yayee
Thank you so much, Sandra, Deyla, Evelyce, Malachi, Kyah, Jill and Yedidah for all of your input into this book.
To all my children and entire family too many to name. I love you all.
Finally, thank you Jesus for placing everything I needed inside of me. We did this!
I know without a shadow of doubt, with you I can do all things.

Michelle would like to thank:
As always, I would like to thank my wonderful husband Joe and to my children, Caleb and Leah, the three best things to ever happen in my life.
To all of the people who have shared their expertise with me so I could share my gifts with the world. This book is, in part, yours. Enjoy the jewels that have been added to your crowns in Heaven because of your kindness. May the Gospel be spread further into the world because of you.
To you, Ruth Langhorn, and to Sandra Gbotoe. Thank you for not pressing the send button and going with someone else on this project! Thank you giving this parched soul the water that she had been lacking for some time. Thank you for listening, for trusting and being obedient to God's calling on your lives. May He multiply your ministry to more than you could ask for or imagine.
Lastly, thank you to my Lord and Savior Jesus Christ. Thank you for choosing me. Thank you for loving me. Thank you for dying for me.

HOW TO USE THIS BOOK

Dolly Parton said, "Discover who you are, then do it on purpose." This is our hope for you as you go on this 60-day journey. As you go through each devotional, take some time to reflect on what the Lord might be saying to you. Then on the lines provided on the opposite page, write down what God is saying. It may be a prayer, a thought, a word or a vision. Feel free to use the reflection questions included at the end of each devotional as a prompt if nothing comes to you. What you hear from God may or may not make sense to you right away—that is OK! Our hope is that this book is something you use over and over again, and God gives you a new revelation every time. If you need someone to go through this with, find someone in your church whom you trust to go through this book alongside of you. You will identify lies the enemy has been telling you, break down walls you have put up around your heart and deepen your relationship with God.

Accept Who You Are

Designed by God

"For just as each of us has one body with many members, and these members do not all have the same function, so in Christ, we, though many, form one body, and each member belongs to all the others"- Romans 12:4-5.

L ooking in the mirror, I had no idea how I changed so much. I didn't recognize the woman standing before me at all. My eyes were red with exhaustion, my hair had not been done in months. I was missing that spark I once had. I was just this shell of a mother, doing what was needed for her kids. Where had my personal identity gone?

One day I realized I had to be more than a mother. Not just for myself but to teach my children the value of putting themselves first. What example would I be to my kids on how to care for themselves if I was not doing it myself? I would have been a hypocrite.

It is imperative that you begin to explore your identity in Christ. There is so much more inside of you than being a mother. I never thought that several businesses or even this devotional book was inside of me. I can't wait to see what else has been hidden out of sight. If I have all these functions inside of me, then I know there so much more in you. Perhaps, you are called to be a lawyer because you perfected the art of defending your children in school. Maybe an author or an alternate newfound career. You could be a doctor helping other little kids stay healthy. There's so much potential that lies inside you. Awaken and see all that God sees in you. Now is the time to explore yourself. Who are you in Christ? What part of the body are you?

Just as there are many parts of the body, there are many parts of you.

Can you imagine the foot functioning without the ankle? How about your hand working without the mobility of your fingers? It doesn't work. This is the same as your purpose only to be a mom; in the same way you have different functions that must work together in order to create a healthy lifestyle. You are a part of the body of Christ; a chosen person. Think about a body, you have your mind that controls the entire body and then you have your heart pumping all your blood through your body so that even the mind gets the blood it needs. How would your body work without the respiratory system getting air to the brain? They all need each other. Just like all these body parts you have a purpose and a function. A mother and caregiver can be absolutely killing it in the mom department while letting every other aspect of herself slip away. Without everything functioning together, there is chaos. This was something that took me a while to figure out.

When I started focusing on my purpose, I spent less time comparing myself to others. Then great things began to happen for me. Everything you need is inside of you because you were perfectly designed by God. Remember He makes no mistakes.

Prayer: *Father, I thank you that you have designed me perfectly in the body of Christ. Help me to function in what you created me to do and never to become complacent or one-dimensional. Amen.*

Reflection Questions

1. When you look in the mirror who or what do you see?

2. Name three gifts that you function quite well in that you may need to begin to explore?

3. What do you believe to be your purpose in life?

Day Two

If God Is for Me, Who Can Be Against Me?

"He answered, 'I heard you in the garden, and I was afraid because I was naked; so I hid'"- Genesis 3:10

A t one of our former churches, we had a couple leave our church because of differences over program and style of our church services. I had nothing against them. That was until we found out they were gossiping about us and slandering our name around town. How could they do that to us? It not only bothered me that the couple left, but I also worried about my reputation, not only as a pastor's wife, but also as a Christian. I worked hard to obey Scripture and maintain my status in the community, and I was concerned the couple would tarnish it.

One morning in prayer, I felt the Lord whisper to my heart, *"Why are you worried about what others think of you? Shouldn't you be more concerned about what I think?"* As I reflected, I realized I cared more about what others thought than what God thought about me. As long as I was innocent in God's eyes, it didn't matter what other people said. Perhaps that couple would execute vengeance on us by ruining our reputation in the community. But once God reassured me that His approval was all that mattered, my fear lifted and was replaced by hope.

Adam and Eve had it all: fellowship, freedom and paradise. They even had God's love and approval free of charge. They didn't have to earn it or work towards it. But with one bite of a seemingly ordinary fruit they lost His unconditional love. Once sin entered the picture, they had to live outside of paradise and outside the parameters of love.

Now they had to work for everything while leaning on each other to meet their needs for love and approval. Sin had blinded them to the reality that they already had all the love and approval they could ever want.

We have all the love we could ever want too. Despite how many friends or significant others you have, there will always be a void that can only be filled with the love of our heavenly father. Don't look for the approval of others, for it is fickle and ever changing. Ask God to fill the void in your heart that only He can fill.

Prayer: *Lord, help us to feel contentment in your approval, and not in the approval of others.*

Reflection Questions

1. Has someone tried to ruin your reputation? If so, how did you handle it?

2. Do you tend to focus more on what others think, or what God thinks?

3. Do you worry about what others think of you? How can you refocus yourself on God's approval?

Comparison and Self-Esteem

"Peter turned and saw that the disciple whom Jesus loved was following them. (This was the one who had leaned back against Jesus at the supper and had said, "Lord, who is going to betray you?") When Peter saw him, he asked, "Lord, what about him?" Jesus answered, "If I want him to remain alive until I return, what is that to you? You must follow me"- John 21:20-21

"Caleb is being mean to me," my daughter said to me when she got off the school bus.

"Why?" I asked.

"Caleb said he's faster than me. He hurt my feelings."

My husband replied, "Well, he is. But who cares? Someone will always be faster, smarter or cooler than you. But that doesn't mean I love you any less."

My daughter walked away with a smile on her face, secure in the love of her father.

It may seem as though self-esteem is a new concept, yet it has been around since after the fall.

Underneath that comparison trap lurks a private yearning to be good enough, worthy enough, to be special and above all others. But what I fail to realize is that in all that wanting, stands the One who already settled my worth a long time ago.

Do you find yourself comparing yourself to others?

Even Peter found himself caught in the trap of comparing himself to the other disciples. Comparison forms an invisible trap between yourself and God. You will always find someone who is prettier, smarter and wealthier than you.

To constantly lust for what others have puts a barrier between you and being grateful for what God has given you.

The antidote for the disease of comparison is contentment. By learning to be content in every circumstance at all times, there leaves no room for comparing yourself to others. There is no need to lust for more because in your mind, you already have it!

Contentment is not easy to achieve. Big name companies make their living off of selling you the feeling you need the biggest, the finest or the best. It's easy to get sucked in to believing the lie that you need something more. Like Eve, our eyes find something appealing, and within seconds, we find ourselves wanting it. It takes self-control to convince yourself you have all you need.

If only Peter had lived secure in Jesus' love for him, especially in his moment of weakness. Accountability could have been key in this situation. Yet, he chose to act on his thoughts and feelings rather than resist the temptation to compare his plight to John's.

Are there weaknesses in your life where you feel inadequate? Do those areas lead you to compare your situation to others?

Comparison can be detrimental to your acceptance of who you are. Accountability and community can help turn your attitude from one of comparison to one of contentment.

Prayer: *Lord, help me to be content with who you are and who you have made me to be.*

Reflection Questions

1. Do you find yourself comparing yourself to others?

2. What areas of your life do you compare yourself to others the most?

3. Why do you think comparison is so easy for women to do?

Less Than or Good Enough?

"You will not certainly die," the serpent said to the woman. *"For God knows that when you eat from it your eyes will be opened, and you will be like God, knowing good and evil"-Genesis 3:4-5.*

Until I knew the Lord, I felt less than. Wearing glasses in middle school, I was automatically dubbed a nerd. My glasses paired with doing well in school, equaled being out of the inner circle of the popular crowds. Because I didn't look like what society believed was good looking, I often felt left out of activities, parties and the inn crowd. From an early age, I equated appearance with worth. Because of this, my *good enough* quickly became *less than*.

Eve struggled with less than, too. Once Satan put doubt in her mind that there was more out there, her good enough world of paradise quickly became less than.

We all struggle with wanting more.

1 Samuel 16:7 says, "But the LORD said to Samuel, "Don't judge by his appearance or height, for I have rejected him. The LORD doesn't see things the way you see them. People judge by outward appearance, but the LORD looks at the heart."

According to this passage, every one of his family thought David was less than. The youngest of his family, everyone overlooked his potential to be king.

Because He didn't look like the ideal candidate, everyone dismissed him. Yet, God saw his heart. He knew the kindness and zeal to obey God that lie deep within David. Because of these qualities, God knew he had what it took to fulfill his royal responsibilities.

David was not chosen because he did everything right. He was loved by God because of who He was. God loves you for who you are, too. Despite what you look like, despite your past, despite how smart you think you are.

Society bases everything on looks. From the newest magazine showcasing the hottest airbrushed model to being judged based on what car you drive, outward appearance is what most people use to determine if someone has worth and value.

But that's not what God uses. God knows your heart. He knows everything you have ever done, ever said, ever thought. He knew you before you were born. He knows your capabilities, even if you feel overlooked by the world. A constant feeling of being overlooked can skew your view of who God is, hindering you from knowing God fully.

God sees everything. He knows you and loves you. When you understand that God judges your worth based on who you are rather than what you look like, you will begin to understand and accept God's love for you.

Prayer: *Lord, allow me to see people's hearts, not their outer appearance.*

Reflection Questions

1. How do you think David felt to be chosen by God as king?

2. Do you feel less than or good enough?

3. How does society's view of who you are change your perception of who you are?

Break Up with Expectations

"And a voice from heaven said, "This is my Son, whom I love; with him I am well pleased"- Matthew 3:17.

I love clocks. I have one in every room of my home. My favorite is one my grandmother had in her home. Growing up, I'd visit her and go into her living room to look at it. I'd open the small door on the bottom, which would unveil all of the moving parts to the clock. I was fascinated with the bushings and springs that all worked together to help the clock keep time. Every hour, it would chime to indicate another hour had passed and a new one had come.

But as I got older, the clock, as all machines do, began to lose time. If I didn't wind the clock every two weeks, it would stop altogether. Frustrated and weary from its unpredictability, I gave up and let the clock sit on the mantel, broken and useless.

I find I view myself this way when it comes to my role as a pastor's wife. Often, when I'm not meeting people's preconceived expectations, they view me like I do that clock: useless. They get frustrated with me because I'm not carrying out the expectations they have planned for me. Yet God has wired me for a specific purpose; **one that changes with time.**

As I grow older, my role shifts given the needs of that specific church. Much like I projected my expectations onto that old clock, people project their expectations onto me.

This can make me feel like I'm not good enough, like God made a mistake in placing me in a high church position.

Jesus didn't get baptized to meet society's expectations.

He got baptized so He could be fully immersed in the work God had called Him to do. When God declares this over His son, He is publicly declaring that He is loved for Who He is; not what He does. Jesus was living for a higher purpose.

I work for a higher purpose and so do you. I live to meet the expectations of the One who responds to my work with "Good job, good and faithful servant." Pursue the plans God has for you; shake off the expectations of others.

Prayer: *Help me not to bow to the expectations of others.*

Reflection Questions

1. What are some expectations others have placed on you?

2. Do you find that you bow to these expectations, for fear you won't be liked?

3. In what ways can you break free from the expectations of others?

Created in God's Image

"So God created man in his own image, in the image of God he created him, male and female he created them"- Genesis 1:27.

G od bestowed on humankind something He gave to no other of His creation: We bear God's image. That doesn't necessarily mean God has human features, but rather we display God's likeness when we go out into the world. Whenever we display a random act of kindness to a stranger, exude patience during an otherwise tense situation and exhibit peace in a situation that would cause panic and unrest, we are displaying God's image to the world.

Yet, it is tough to decipher who God really is when Christians don't act in accordance with what the Bible teaches. It's easy to give up on God when God's people are embroiled in battle with an unbelieving world touting their views on social media about hot button cultural topics instead of loving others the way God would love them.

Bear in mind, this verse in Genesis occurred before the fall, when everything was perfect. This was God's intention. God wanted to be in direct communication with his creation so He, along with Jesus and the Holy Spirit, guide and direct His children throughout their lives. However, after the fall, man chose to go his own way. No longer was God the ultimate guide. The separation of God and man due to the sin nature now makes it more necessary to be the walking talking example of Christ a world desperately wants to see.

Like a radio with bad reception, our communication with God is a bit fuzzy and makes it difficult to hear from Him clearly.

But it doesn't have to be that way forever. God created Adam with a partner in community so He didn't have to walk alone in His journey, and neither do you. God has placed in your path many modes of increasing your communication with Him. You may not know how to fully bear his image yet, but my prayer is that through improving your relationships with other brothers and sisters in Christ, discovering your spiritual gifts and pinpointing ways to increase your communication with God, you will begin to see yourself (and your life) in a new way, and your understanding of how to bear the image of God will become natural to you.

Prayer: *Help me become a part of a community that will guide me in my spiritual life.*

Discussion Questions

Have you ever heard that God created you to bear His image? If so, what do you think that meant?

What difference do you think it makes that God made that statement before the fall?

What are the implications of the fall on how we bear the image of God today?

Self- Stewardship

"Teacher, which is the greatest commandment in the Law?" Jesus replied: "'Love the Lord your God with all your heart and with all your soul and with all your mind.' This is the first and greatest commandment. And the second is like it: 'Love your neighbor as yourself'- Matthew 22:35-39.

Loving your neighbor as yourself may seem unachievable especially to those who don't deserve it. It's a pretty strong command yet it's obtainable. This is not the kind of love that is selfish or inwardly focused. It ultimately results in outward focus. Loving your neighbor is not narcissistic, but biblically necessary. This is not primarily for your gain but for God's glory. The joy, blessings, and rewards are secondary and a byproduct of stewarding self. It's all for His glory and purposes. We must begin stewarding well our spirit, mind, body, heart and soul for the glory of God and the service of others.

As mothers, we are givers by nature and we love with all our hearts. Of course, loving our neighbor which could represent our family, children and friends comes quite easy. Yet, we tend to fail in the area of self-care which is a pre-requisite of loving yourself. I am just coming to the realization that self- care is not selfish but stewardship of our bodies, souls and minds. Good stewardship of God's love begins with godly self-stewardship of oneself.

God has given us a tremendous amount of capital to steward well for his Kingdom, and it starts with loving Him enough to love ourselves. Let's commit to godly self-stewardship for the glory of God and the good of others.

Prayer: *Heavenly Father, I will be more intentional when it comes to self-care activities, like taking better care of myself and my nails, by going to get coffee, or treating myself to a movie. Thank you for teaching me that by loving you it will help me love others as much as I love myself. I love you with all of my heart. Amen.*

Reflection Questions

1. Are you examining your daily routine to identify personal self-care practices?

2. Do you find it hard to take time out for you?

3. List 3 ways you can be more intentional about treating yourself better?

God Looks at the Heart

"But the LORD said to Samuel, "Don't judge by his appearance or height, for I have rejected him. The LORD doesn't see things the way you see them. People judge by outward appearance, but the LORD looks at the heart."-1 Samuel 16:7.

Society bases everything on looks. From the newest magazine showcasing the hottest airbrushed model to being judged based on what car you drive, outward appearance is what most people use to determine if someone has worth and value.

David was not chosen because He did everything right. He was loved by God because of who He was. God loves you for who you are, too. Despite what you look like, despite your past, despite how smart you think you are.

But that's not what God uses. God knows your heart. He knows everything you have ever done, ever said, ever thought. He knew you before you were born. He knows your capabilities, even of you feel overlooked by the world. A constant feeling of being overlooked can skew your view of who God is, hindering you from knowing God fully.

God sees everything. He knows you and loves you. When you understand that God judges your worth based on who you are rather than what you look like, you will begin to understand and accept God's love for you.

Prayer: *Lord, help me to see myself the way you see me.*

Reflection Questions

1. How do you think David felt to be chosen by God as king?

2. Do you feel less than or good enough?

3. How does society's view of who you are change your perception of who you are?

The Deception of the False Self

"You will not surely die," the serpent told her. "For God knows that in the day you eat of it, your eyes will be opened and you will be like God, knowing good and evil." Genesis 3:4-5.

In my previous devotion, I wrote about getting glasses. Initially excited, I chose a pair of lavender colored glasses, my favorite color. I couldn't wait until I got to school to show off my new specs.

That was until I got my first taste of ridicule. People talking behind my back calling me a nerd was devastating. Being told I was a nerd because of my glasses made me wear the contact lenses I received when I was sixteen every day, never to let anyone see me with my glasses. Recently, however, I have noticed that a nagging dry eye paired with flimsy contact lenses has forced me to wear my glasses more often, even out in public. I thought my first run in with someone I knew at the grocery store would cause me great embarrassment, wanting to duck into the produce aisle and avoid the acquaintance until they left the store. But I felt eerily confident and talked to the person with ease. When they left, I wasn't embarrassed at all; in fact, it felt a bit freeing.

Being known for who you truly are without the need to cover yourself up is restoring the freedom Adam and Eve had with God. It's the freedom He intended us to have, to approach Him for who we truly are, holding nothing back, and allowing God to love you for just as you are.

If I had worried less about what others thought and more about what God thought, I might have been happier with who I was. But I internalized those remarks, allowing it to affect the whole of who I was.

This caused me to wear contact lenses in public, make-up on my face and trendy clothes on my body, in an effort to cover-up who I was.

When we put on a false self to others instead of being who we are, we want to cover up who we are instead of exposing ourselves to others. We believe a lie that who we are is not good enough.

Adam and Eve believed this too. The serpent made Eve believe that there was more out there, including a better life than what she already had. This made her eyes and heart lust after more, forsaking the life God had given her. Instead of understanding she was thriving, the serpent deceived her into thinking she was merely surviving.

False selves can deceive us too. It deceives others into believing you are someone you are not, and it deceives you into believing your worth comes from places other than God.

Embrace your weaknesses as well as your strengths. Be proud of who you are, knowing that everyone has flaws. Don't try to be perfect but live in the reality that perfection is a myth. This is the first step in leaving your false self behind and embracing your real self.

Prayer: Lord, help me to know who I truly am so I can resist the temptation to be someone I am not.

Reflection Questions

1. Think for a moment about a time when you were ridiculed because of outward appearance. How did that make you feel?

2. Did those remarks impact who you are now? Did it impact you positively or negatively?

3. What is one action step you could take to forsake your false self and embracing your real self?

Taking off the Mask

"Then the eyes of both of them were opened, and they realized they were naked"-
Genesis 3:7.

As I hopped out of the shower to get ready for the day, I dressed in my prettiest top and pants and prepared to embark on my daily beauty regimen of putting on my makeup. I applied my foundation like a painter applying a coat of primer, careful to cover every flaw and imperfection from the naked eye. As I worked, I felt God gently whisper to my heart:

Why do you need to cover your flaws? You are beautiful in spite of your flaws.

Like many women, I believed the lie that my worth is based on my physical appearance, not on my inward characteristics. In response, I took my washcloth and washed it all off. Then I went to church. You know what happened?

Nothing.

No one commented on my lack of makeup. No one criticized my seemingly unkempt appearance.

I realized that I was using my makeup not only as a physical technique to cover my imperfections, but I also used it like a mask to pretend that I had it all together. Deep down, if people saw my flaws, they might not like me as a person. What a terrifying feeling! But even more terrifying is not being who God has made me to be. When I put my worth in Christ and not in others' perceptions of me, what people think of me becomes less important.

Perhaps you can relate. Maybe you don't wear makeup, but maybe you use other areas of life as a mask to cover up your insecurities. Maybe you use clothing tricks to cover your body's trouble zones. Perhaps you use food or drinks to medicate from the pain your past has caused. But God wants us as His disciples to take off the masks in our lives and let the world see who we truly are.

Prayer: *Lord, help us to take off our masks and allow ourselves to be accepted for who we are. Amen.*

Reflection Questions

1. Do you use your make-up as a way of covering up your physical imperfections?

2. Make-up is a tangible item used to cover up the physical parts of us, but also serves as a metaphor for the inner flaws we try to cover up from the world. What inner behaviors, thoughts or feelings do you not want the world to see?

3. What mental, emotional and spiritual work do you need to do on the inside so you can feel free to face the world without make-up?

Where Is Your Identity?

"Now the LORD God had formed out of the ground all the wild animals and all the birds in the sky. He brought them to the man to see what he would name them; and whatever the man called each living creature, that was its name. So, the man gave names to all the livestock, the birds in the sky and all the wild animals" Genesis 2:19-20.

Recently attending a women's event, I registered at the welcome desk and stepped to the side. "Please write your name on the nametag," the woman pointed as she slid a sticker towards me. I wrote my name in big letters and slapped it on my chest. I entered the auditorium and sat down in one of the front rows. I waited the full forty- five minutes before the event began, looking around while haphazardly looking at my phone. People filed into the seats in front of me and behind me. But no one said anything to me. I smiled at the people filing in, and they smiled back, but no one asked anything about me. No one asked who I was or where I lived. It was like I was invisible.

Before I pursued an intimate relationship with Jesus at age eighteen, my identity was wrapped up in how many friends I had, what designer clothes were on my body and what grades appeared on my report card. But all of those things don't define who I am, Christ's love does. Yet, identity is something every human struggles with throughout her life.

Adam and Eve had identity issues, too. The animals and everything created up to this point had been God's. Yet in this moment, He partners with Adam and gives him the sole responsibility of naming the animals. He allows Adam to identify with Him as a co –creator. What's Adam's first job? Giving the animals their identity through their name. Adam can truly identify with God through participating in His work.

We fight that tension as much today as Adam and Eve did back then. The world pressures us to identify with it when we act like it. But we choose to identify with God when we separate ourselves from the world through actions that please God rather than displease Him. However, we often serve and lead in churches to feed our own need for significance rather than living in the knowledge that our worth was settled on the cross long ago.

When we don't fully understand and accept our Father's love, we look for other outlets to fill that need instead. We look for ways to fill the voids in our lives through counterfeit versions of wholeness.

Prayer: *Help me find my identity in you and nowhere else.*

Reflection Questions

1. In what ways do you fill the voids in your life through counterfeit wholeness?

2. How can you use your work to identify yourself as a co- creator with God?

3. How can you separate yourself from the world so you can more clearly identify yourself with God?

Understand Your Authority

A Daughter of the King

See what great love the Father has lavished on us, that we should be called children of God! And that is what we are- 1 John 3:1

Two kids. Feedings every three hours. Staring at the mounds of dirty diapers in the garbage pail and mounds of dirty dishes in the sink, it seemed life was one meaningless task after another. Graduating with my Master's Degree, I thought life was going to involve me going into counseling. I imagined my life so much more different than it turned out to be. Two years and two children later, one thought raced through my mind:

Is there more to life than this?

As women, it is easy to become wrapped up in our to-do lists, allowing loads of laundry and mounds of dishes to undermine our positions as daughters of the King. The world we live in will make us feel small, reducing our purpose in the Kingdom to mundane tasks and boring existences. Yet, we are royalty! God has adopted us as His daughters through Christ's death on the cross. Once we live in the realization that we have access to God's throne just by asking and understanding the authority God has given us as his daughters, it will shift our perspective and help us to live purposeful, meaningful lives.

Lord, help me to know whose I am. Remind me of my position as a daughter of the king. Don't allow my seemingly mundane experiences to overshadow my worth in you. Amen.

Prayer: *Lord, remind me daily that I am a daughter of the King.*

Reflection Questions

1. In what ways can you remind yourself you are a daughter of the King?

2. Do you think your circumstances derail you from remembering who you are as royalty?

3. What do you think God means when you hear you are adopted into God's family?

Day Thirteen
Approach God with Boldness

"So, let us come boldly to the throne of our gracious God. There we will receive his mercy, and we will find grace when we need it most"- Hebrews 4:16.

In 2012, I had what I thought was a urinary tract infection. Besides feeling tired and a dull ache, it didn't bother me much. I took over the counter medications, but it didn't help much. One night, however, the pain had spread to the point where I was in so much pain I couldn't sit, lie down or even stand. Panicked, I drove myself to the emergency room. I thought I was going to die! After a false diagnosis of a bladder infection, it took almost two full weeks to heal. Seeing my regular physician, he eventually diagnosed me with cystitis which is more of a chronic condition. Although I was glad to have a diagnosis, I constantly had a relative amount of discomfort all the time.

I didn't know what was going on with me; but I knew someone who did. So, I got down on my knees and closed my eyes:

Lord, I need your help. What I'm feeling is not right. Something is wrong and I need to know what it is. I need your spirit's revelation to help me understand what it is. Please show me what is wrong so I can get medicine and not allow it to affect my ministry to others.

Suddenly, I got the idea to start monitoring my diet and reading labels. I quickly realized all the foods I ate before the discomfort returned contained wheat or soy. I eliminated the foods from my diet, and guess what? The discomfort went away! Doctors couldn't diagnose it. Friends couldn't help me.

But the power of the Spirit's revelation gave me the information and grace I needed to change my ways and lead a pain free life.

It was all because I boldly approached God's throne and asked Him.

Prayer: *Lord, help us learn what it means to approach you boldly with our requests. Help us not to give up when the answers don't come as quickly as we'd like.*

Reflection Questions

1. Is there an area in your life you would like to see the Lord heal?

2. What stops you from approaching God with boldness?

3. Do you have a story where God gave you mercy and grace simply because you asked him for it? What happened?

God Used His Hands

"Then the LORD God formed a man from the dust of the ground and breathed into his nostrils the breath of life, and the man became a living being."- Genesis 2:7.

One of my favorite memories of my son was the morning ritual I had established when I would retrieve him from his crib in the morning. Each morning, I opened the door slowly, greeted by the soothing sounds of a lullaby CD I would play each night. I would approach his crib, and my son would be entertaining himself with the toy hanging on one of the crib railings. He'd touch every button, turn every knob and look at himself in the mirror. Sometimes he was so engrossed in what he was doing, he would not notice my presence for several minutes. Once he caught a glimpse of me in the mirror, he'd turn around and smile his biggest smile. He'd arise and allow me to scoop him up into my arms. Then he'd put his head on my right shoulder and I'd rub his back and sway back and forth, singing sweetly in his ear. Then I'd put him down to allow him to barrel out the door and into the rest of the house, eager to start his busy day.

I easily could have greeted him with a word, alerting him to my presence. But instead I'd allow us to bond over the gift of my touch. A gentle rub on the back as he placed his head on my shoulder, basking in the bond of a mother with her son.

Up until this point in Genesis, God spoke things into being. He declared, "Let there be…" and it was so. But with humans it was different. God chose to use his hands and interact with mankind through human touch as he formed a man from dust. God used His hands to create Adam and Eve, not something He did with any part of creation.

Maybe it was to add an extra measure of care human life, to place humans higher in the hierarchy of life. Maybe he wanted to appreciate the same bond with His children as I did with my son. Human contact and touch are necessary to a baby's thriving. Hospitals often allow volunteers to hold abandoned babies just to help them thrive. Husbands and wives deepen their level of intimacy when they hold hands, kiss and engage in intercourse.

As women, we crave intimacy as well. We all want to bond with a special person in our lives to give our lives meaning and value. Where this gets skewed is when we lower our standards to meet our needs for intimacy at the expense of our value. We choose men who are less than our best simply because we haven't fully understood our worth and value in God. If God took time out of His work of creating to bond with us through touch, then how much more would it be worth it for us to examine ourselves and set high standard in the mates we choose?

Choosing someone who is of high moral standing and treats us the way we should be treated is not being picky, it's knowing our Father wouldn't want anything less for us.

Prayer: *Lord, help me discover (and maintain) my worth in you.*

Reflection Questions

1. Why do you think God used his hands to create mankind?
2.
3. Have you ever chosen a mate who was less than what you deserved?

4. Why do you think you stayed in the relationship?

Day Fifteen

Shameless Audacity

I tell you, even though he will not get up and give you the bread because of friendship, yet because of your shameless audacity he will surely get up and give you as much as you need. So I say to you: Ask and it will be given to you; seek and you will find; knock and the door will be opened to you. For everyone who asks receives; the one who seeks finds; and to the one who knocks, the door will be opened- Luke 11:8-10.

The Christian life has not been easy for me. The road to my spiritual journey has been laced with trials, persecution and loss. Although I would do it all over again if I had the chance, there have been times when I have clung to my faith in God to get me through tough times.

But if I'm honest, I don't pray like I should without wanting to quit. When my prayers are not answered in my time frame or in the way I think they should, I quit. I assume the answer is no and I give up altogether, convinced that continuing to pray is a waste of my time.

But in the above passage, the man received what he asked for (the bread) simply because God is good and provides as much as His children need. God promises He will answer the door if we knock and give to us because we ask. It may take longer than we anticipate, but if we persevere and continue to ask, God will be faithful in answering us.

Prayer: *Lord, help us to pray to you with shameless audacity. If the answer doesn't come as quickly as we would like, help us to keep knocking on the doors of heaven, clinging to the promise you will open it and meet us there.*

Reflection Questions

1. 1. Do you keep asking the Lord for your requests or do you give up because they are not answered in your timeframe?

2. What prayers has God answered because you chose not to give up?

3. What area of your life would you like to keep praying for until God provides for it? Write it at the top of the journal section on the opposite

page. Look at it regularly as a reminder to pray for it. Write all the ways God has answered your prayers in that area.

Walk in Your Authority

"I have given you authority to trample on snakes and scorpions and to overcome all the power of the enemy; nothing will harm you" Luke 10:19.

A t a ladies' retreat where I was the main speaker, the time came for me to speak on the role of the church in each other's lives. Out of the four sessions I had planned, this one was my favorite. I have come to love the church. One of the desires of my heart is to see the members of Christ's body sharpening and loving each other and caring for each other's needs. This was also the session that I was going to conclude with communion and healing. I wasn't sure how well these acts were going to be received. But I wanted to be obedient to the call I felt God was placing on me for that night. I opened my black binder that held the notes I had carefully typed onto my note paper. I began to speak with the same enthusiasm as I had when I spoke at the ladies' retreat for my own church.

About halfway through the session, the air in the room changed.

Nothing appeared different. But it felt different. It felt lighter, almost like it was easier to breathe. I proceeded to try to speak the next words on the page, but I couldn't. Suddenly, I felt a sense to turn from the original text and go to a completely different passage in my Bible. I had just studied it in a Bible study I had attended the week before, and it had special significance to me. Little did I know that at that Bible study God was preparing me for the experience that was about to unfold before my eyes in just a moment.

I informed the audience that I felt God was directing me to another passage.

I assured them that I had prepared for this session, but I was being directed elsewhere. The new direction flustered me a bit and I struggled to find my words. The awkward pause made people a bit antsy. Then one woman whispered, "The spirit is moving." I replied, "Yes, He is." I asked them to turn to John 5, which is the passage about the healing of the blind man at the pool.

I read the passage and pointed out that the most discouraging thing about the passage was that there was a whole community around him, yet no one dared help the man. Jesus saw the need of one man and met the need. Jesus then found the man at the temple, and then and only then convicted him of his sin and moved him toward repentance.

At this point I was crying and I asked them, "Are you willing to get up and meet the needs of those around you?" I also challenged them to analyze how they were treating the youth, the next generation of people. I then said that that is the reason why the youth are not flocking to churches anymore. The church has not made them feel welcome to eat at God's "banquet table."

I then turned to Luke 14, the story of God inviting those around to come eat at the banquet table, but the people are all busy. He asks the people to find the poor, lame, weak, etc., and keep inviting them until the banquet table was full. I then ushered them into a time of communion. I challenged them to take the bread and cup and to serve it to each other. I asked them to look past the religious affiliations of the person next to them and asked them to focus on the servant aspect of communion.

After a time of quiet meditation, and the wiping away of a few tears, I felt it was time to enter into a time of healing. I let them know that I had not planned this, but that God had asked me to do this. I said I brought a small container of olive oil and that if anyone wanted to come up to the front, I would lay hands on them and pray for them.

I sat down and waited, swinging my legs like a nervous school girl, waiting for the principal to call me into his office.

I expected no one to come up, that even though I wanted to be obedient to God's calling, I had somehow gotten it all wrong. Then, it happened. Someone came up. I told them I didn't know what I was doing but that I would pray and ask God that if He wanted to heal and use me as his vessel to do it, then I would do it. So, I prayed. I thought that that would be it and it would all be over. Then, someone else came up. And another. And another.

Soon, the pastor's wife and other women came up and joined me in praying for whoever was in need. People started praying out loud. They prayed for forgiveness for the mistreatment of the youth in this country, and praying for one another's needs, even those who weren't there at the retreat.

It was one of the most extraordinary moments of my life as a follower of Christ. But, even as these wonderful things were taking place, a war was raging in my mind. Satan was doing battle in my mind. It wasn't incredible, but subtle.

Thoughts such as, the pastor is going to be so mad when he finds out and I can't heal them, I don't have the gift, and people are going to think this was set up from the beginning. I never expressed these doubts publicly, but every time I would place my hand on someone, the thoughts would begin. My sister-in-law even came down, asking to be healed from some issues she had been struggling with for some time. I have firmly believed for a while now that demons had been tormenting her mind for a long time.

However, I never had the opportunity to pray for her or to cast them out as Scripture dictates until now. The opportunity arose, and I took it. I was scared of what would happen, the outcome after I did it, and by what authority I had to do it. But, I did it. I wasn't going to let the opportunity for God to use me in this way pass me by. I was willing, and I think God honored my willingness. For almost two hours this continued. Although the Spirit was moving mightily, the time came for us to conclude. The pastor's wife stood up and tried to wrap us up and direct us to the next activity on the agenda.

As we started mingling again, a woman came up to me and said "here, this is for you. As I was praying, God wanted me to give this to you."

I thought "Here we go. Let the persecution begin. She's mad at me that I did this because it is against their service style and theological views. I'm doomed." Nevertheless, I opened up the large white notebook paper folded into threes. This is what the note said:

Michelle,

God bless you for your willing obedience to Him. May He strengthen you daily as you walk in the authority given to you in Jesus' name.

Even as I write this today, chills run down my spine. I have yet to have an encounter with God since that retreat that has come close to rivaling it. If Jesus had walked out of the bathroom Himself and handed me the note personally, I would not have been surprised.

If I had understood and walked in my authority that day, there would have been no need for me to be fearful that day. God has given me the authority do the things He did when He was here on earth. He has given you that same authority. We just need to walk in it.

Prayer: *Lord, help me to walk daily in the authority you gave me as your child.*

Reflection Questions

1. Do you understand the authority God has given you as your child?

2. Does the idea you have authority to heal, drive out demons and spread the Gospel scare you?

3. In what ways can you learn to walk daily in this God given authority?

Deepen Your Relationship
With God

Making the Better Choice: Choosing Worship Over Work

We all know the story. Two sisters in the presence of Jesus with two completely different reactions: One allows herself to get distracted by the cares of preparing a meal, one basks in the glory of the savior.

Personally, I like Martha. Martha's one of my favorite people in the Bible. Perhaps it is because she is a workhorse like me or perhaps it's because she tells Jesus like it is: "Lord, don't you care that my sister has left me to do the work by myself? Tell her to help me! (Luke 10:40)." Whatever the case, I've always thought Martha got the short end of the stick when it came to Jesus' gentle rebuke. That was, until I recently reread the passage again. I noticed something about Jesus' words to her: he never reprimands her for working! He only asks her not to allow the worries of the work to overwhelm her to the point of losing her focus on what is truly important.

Work is a good thing! God created work so that we can fulfill our purpose here on earth. However, in our task-oriented society, we often make to-do lists and plug along in our day, forgetting about the relationships and people God has placed in our lives.

How do we find our balance between a hard day's work and adequate time to rest and fix our eyes on Jesus?

1) "But few things are needed—or indeed only one"—Jesus wants us to enjoy all aspects of our lives, including work and worship. Once we put Jesus first in our lives, everything else flows from it, including our work.
2) "Mary has chosen what is better"—Worship is a choice. Mary chose to make use of what little time she had at Jesus' feet rather than in the kitchen. Martha, however, chose to allow the details of her dinner to overwhelm her. God wants us to choose Him over completing our tasks.
3) "It will not be taken from her"—Jesus makes a choice, too. He chooses not to honor Martha's request of asking Mary to help Martha. When we choose to focus on our relationship with God rather than our tasks, God honors us by giving us the strength and perseverance to get our work done.

Prayer: *Lord, help us make the better choice of spending time with you rather than checking off our to-do list. Amen.*

Reflection Questions

1. Are you a Martha or a Mary? Do you spend more time checking off your to-do list than you do spending time with God?

2. Do you dread your work, or do you see it as an act of worship?

3. If you dread your work, in what ways can you shift your perspective to one of worshipping at your work?

Our Deepest Desires

"When the woman saw that the fruit of the tree was good for food and pleasing to the eye, and also desirable for gaining wisdom, she took some and ate it" Genesis 2:4.

I have a confession to make: I like when people give me encouragement. I am willing to bet you do, too. There is nothing wrong with encouragement, as long as it remains within the confines of building up a brother or sister in Christ. The problem becomes when I am constantly looking for it. If I'm posting pictures on my social media sites just so someone will click the "like" button, my need for encouragement is coming from the wrong place. That was Adam and Eve's problem. Eve didn't know she wanted to live independently from God until Satan enlightened her that there was something she was missing. Once she realized she could have "her eyes opened," that was when her desires kicked in. Before the fall, there was nothing to desire because they had everything they could ever want because God had provided them with everything they could ever need. Soon the desire consumed Eve's heart and mind, which soon translated into her desire being fulfilled by eating the apple.

Desires are a natural part of our life. But when we desire material possessions or needs that fill our empty souls instead of going to God, that's when our desires turn inappropriate. Notice that her desires are attached to the lies Satan told her. If she had stood on the truth that God had given Adam when He placed him in the garden, she could have thwarted the devil's evil schemes and returned to paradise.

Desires are not bad, but they have to be in the proper perspective. If your desires are tied to glorifying yourself, they don't benefit you or God.
But if they give glory to God, more than likely God will grant it. It may be difficult to discern if your desire benefits you or God, but that's where your connection with Him plays an important role. If you remain in God, He will give you the desires of your heart.

All you have to do is ask.

Prayer: *Lord, help my desires to line up with your will.*

Reflection Questions

1. Do your desires line up with God's will for your life? Why or why not?

2. Which desires must you rid yourself of to more closely align with God's will?

3. Do you believe desires are a part of God's plan for us? Explain.

Huffing and Puffing My Way to the Finish Line

"Therefore, since we are surrounded by such a great cloud of witnesses, let us throw off everything that hinders and the sin that so easily entangles. And let us run with perseverance the race marked out for us" Hebrews 12:1.

A s I put on my workout clothes and began stretching my body, I stared out the window and sighed. It rained non-stop over the past few weeks. It would be easy to make excuses as to why I couldn't go out and run.

The ground is too wet.

I'm too tired.

I can do it tomorrow.

I had been working hard; I can make it up next week.

No one would have known if I had forsaken my commitment to train for a 5k. But I'd know and sometimes I'm the hardest person to disappoint.

It's the same in my life as a disciple. The busyness of life sometimes keeps me from regular devotion time. One week turns into two weeks, two weeks into a month, and then soon I can't remember how long it's been since I had spent time alone with God. In the same way, I want to make excuses rather than run each day to train for a 5k. It's always easier to make excuses instead of doing the hard work of discipleship. But if I do the work each day of studying the word of God, practicing disciplines like silence and fasting, my faith stretches and grows. Just like each half hour I dedicate to running, my lung capacity grows, too.

It's hard, much like life. But when I'm huffing and puffing my way to the finish line when my training is over, the still small voice tells me to keep going, because although the tough times may seem long, they soon give way to perseverance and hope.

And that's what makes it all worth it.

Prayer: Lord, give us the endurance to stretch our spiritual growth so we may reach the finish line. Amen.

Reflection Questions

1. Do you make excuses for your spiritual life as to why you don't work on it regularly?

2. In what ways do you need to stretch and grow your faith?

3. What role do you think spiritual disciplines (like silence, writing in a journal and fasting) can help you grow in your faith?

It's the Little Things

"From everyone who has been given much, much will be demanded; and from the one who has been entrusted with much, much more will be asked."- Luke 12:48.

Yesterday I started training for a 5K (although I didn't start out my day thinking that way.)

A group of friends gathered at the local park to run or walk. I have always wanted to train for a 5K but have never been able to muster the stamina or lung capacity to do so. When I arrived, I didn't expect to start training. In fact, I didn't know what to expect. We all decided to follow the schedule for couch to 5K running program. I was apprehensive; convinced I would have to quit.

But with each cycle, you know what I found? It got a little easier, simply because I showed up, put one foot in front of the other and committed to completing the goal. I finished day one of the program. But that was day one. I have many days to go.

If I expect to cross the finish line of a 5K, I have to show up, commit to doing the work and give God what I have, even if it's the little things. Matthew 1:15-18 (NIV) says: As evening approached, the disciples came to him and said, "This is a remote place, and it's already getting late. Send the crowds away, so they can go to the villages and buy themselves some food." Jesus replied, "They do not need to go away. You give them something to eat." "We have here only five loaves of bread and two fish," they answered. "Bring them here to me," he said.

If I agree to give God the little things I have to offer, He will take it and multiply it to His glory for the purpose of changing lives.

Prayer: *Lord, help me put one foot in front of the other in my spiritual life. Help me persevere until I reach the finish line.*

Reflection Questions

1. What "little thing" do you need to give over to God?

2. Are there times in your spiritual life when you want to quit?

3. Why were the disciples so nervous about the amount of food being enough to feed the crowds?

A Little Bit of Coffee and a Whole Lot of Jesus

"Jesus answered, 'Everyone who drinks this water will be thirsty again, but whoever drinks the water I give them will never thirst. Indeed, the water I give them will become in them a spring of water welling up to eternal life.'"- John 4:11, 13.

I've got to hurry; the kids are going to be late for school!

Hopping into the shower, I used the bathroom towel to wipe the sweat off of my brow from my workout. I washed quickly, still making sure I cleaned every area. Grabbing the snacks from the pantry, I threw them into a plastic bag and handed them to my kids who plopped them into their backpacks. Opening the screen door, we all headed to the bus stop. When I got home, I grabbed the eggs from the fridge and scrambled them up, flipping them in the frying pan until the liquid yolk turned a golden color. I scooped the fluffy eggs onto my plate and placed the pan and spatula in the sink. I poured some water into a nearby glass from the gallon of water in the fridge. I wiped my hands on the dishtowel and looked down to read the words scrawled on the front of the towel.

This is what it said:

What I need today is a little coffee and a whole lot of Jesus.

Jesus. In my hustle and bustle of the day, I had forgotten to commune with Jesus. In fact, spending time with Jesus never even crossed my mind. Consumed with filling my earthly stomach, I failed to nourish my soul by breaking bread with Him and drinking from His living water.

Isn't this true of all of us? Why do we choose to shortchange the power of God's transformative power in our live by substituting for a counterfeit? Why do we choose to go our own way when our Heavenly Father wants us to merely sit with Him and drink?

Prayer: *Father, help us not to choose to go our own way but to choose to commune with you.*

Reflection Questions

1. Why do we rebel from God when what He gives us is sufficient for us?

2. Why is it hard to commune with Jesus?

3. In what ways can we commune with Jesus outside of the bread and juice we take together in church?

Abide in Christ

"If anyone does not abide in me, he is thrown away as a branch and dries up; and they gather them and cast them into the fire and they are burned. "If you abide in me, and my words abide in you, ask whatever you wish, and it will be done for you. "My Father is glorified by this, that you bear much fruit, and so prove to be my disciples"- John 15:6-8.

I've read these verses many times in Scripture, but the word "abide" has always eluded me. It's not a word in common, everyday language, so it's a word I'm not so familiar with. So, what does it mean to "abide?"

In Greek the word *abide* is a word that means to "remain" or "wait." In other words, it means to wait upon or with. So how do we constantly wait or remain in the Lord?

If we don't abide in Christ, it is like we are willing to throw away our lives on things that don't matter. When we try to live apart from Christ, our lives suffer. If we amass wealth or take care of our fragile bodies with no purpose or only for personal gain, our lives mean nothing. If we try to teach our children to have good manners and live a good life apart from Christ, how will they be different from the rest of the world, and how will they be able to further the Gospel here on earth?

One of the ways we can abide in Christ when we feel God is being silent is to cling to each other in all facets of our lives. In our individualistic world, it is easy to attempt to do the Christian life alone. Yet, we can do nothing apart from Christ. We need each other and the Lord to cling to moment by moment, day by day. As women, we need to bond together as women and lean on each other during both the highs and lows of our lives so we don't have to feel as if we are alone.

If we abide in Christ, and each other, we will bear fruit— fruit that edifies us (patience, goodness, kindness and the like) and that the world desires.

Prayer: *Lord, help us to abide in Christ and each other so we can reap the abundant life Christ promised.*

Reflection Questions

1. Do you feel alone in your spiritual walk? What have you done in your own strength to remedy this?

2. In what ways can we abide in Christ?

3. How do you think clinging to other sisters in Christ will help you to abide in Him?

Walk in Courage

Day Twenty-Three

The Lord Is Your Shield

"After this, the word of the Lord *came to Abram in a vision: "Do not be afraid, Abram. I am your shield, your very great reward."'* - Genesis 15:1.

I'm a control freak. I love the predictability of routine and when life goes the way I planned. The problem with this is that in my finite abilities, I don't know what is around the corner for me. I don't know if the doctor is going to have good news or bad news when he calls with my test results. I don't know what's in the envelope when my kids bring one home from school. I also don't know whether or not that call from my dad will be his last.

But I know someone who does know.

According to this verse, the Lord is my shield. In times of war, shields are used to protect warriors from the fiery darts of the enemy. In my life, the Lord protects me from the darts of my enemy, the devil. When it comes to my relationship with the Lord, I forget that God already knows what will happen before I do. He goes before me, protecting me from situations that might bring me harm. When I forget this, I fear that God will allow me to endure difficulties that will lead to my harm. But God has plans to bring good to my life, even if it comes in the form of a trial or difficult situation.

He goes before me. He protects me. When I rest in this, I have nothing to fear.

Prayer: *Lord, help me to rest in the knowledge that you are our protector, shielding us from the fiery darts of the enemy.*

Reflection Questions
1. Do you live in the knowledge that God goes before you, protecting you from the difficulties of life?

2. Do you trust in God's provision or do you like to control your circumstances?

3. In what ways do you need to trust God more and control your life less?

You Are Not Alone

"Have I not commanded you? Be strong and courageous. Do not be afraid; do not be discouraged, for the LORD *your God will be with you wherever you go."- Joshua 1:9*

When I was a little girl, I was afraid of the dark. Like most kids, I'd cower in the corner of my bed, hanging on to whatever light I could muster from the moonlight streaming into my window. Every noise I'd hear I immediately believed was an ominous monster hiding in my closet, ready to attack at any moment. I'd pray that God would protect me and keep me safe from those monsters. I'd fall asleep to those prayers, awakened to a new day and a new chance to play and explore the world around me. The monsters I feared lurking in my closet became nothing but figments of my imagination by day, but at night, would morph back into those hideous, menacing creatures.

I'm sure Joshua felt this way when he had to face some of the menacing enemies of his day. But he wasn't alone. Not only did he have Caleb, a faithful servant leader, by his side to walk along with him, but he also had God, who promised to be with him no matter what happened.

Adam and Eve got their first taste of fear in the Garden, too. Although it wasn't God's intention for them to be afraid, they must have experienced some fear, or else why would they want to hide themselves from God? They had no reason to fear Him before the Fall. But once their eyes were opened, they began to see God, and Eden differently. Soon they worried about what God might say to them once He discovered they had disobeyed.

It is the same with us today. So often we allow our biggest fears to become menacing, terrifying creatures, too. But having a friend to help you along your spiritual walk helps us to understand we are not alone.

Prayer: *Lord, help us to find a spiritual friend that will reassure us we are not alone.*

Reflection Questions

1. What were you afraid of as a child that you aren't afraid of now? Why are those fears not as frightening now as an adult?

2. What fears do you have that seemed big at one time but when you shine light on them seem small and irrational?

3. Has God placed someone in your path that can walk alongside of you in your spiritual journey?

The Spiritual and Emotional Rest We All Need

"As far as it depends on you, live at peace with everyone"-Romans 12:18.

Being a pastor's wife is not easy. As a leader in my church, sometimes I have to confront people in their sin, requiring me to engage in conflict. Sometimes this results in people leaving the church. It's never easy and can be downright heart breaking, as church members feel like they are a part of my extended family. But the hardest part is not *during* the conflict; it is *after* a conflict when I see that person who has left for the first time. It is so awkward, especially if the other party is still holding a grudge. When I see that person, even if I haven't done anything wrong, my heart races, my palms sweat, and my mind runs with memories of the hurtful exchange. The enemy points his accusatory finger, tricking me into believing I will have that conflict again.

The New Testament is clear that as long as I have done all I can to resolve the conflict and ask for forgiveness when necessary, I no longer have to fear seeing the person again. I sleep well at night knowing my conscience is clear and that I have done the right thing, even when it is difficult.

I get physical rest because my heart and soul are at rest, too.

Prayer: *Lord, for those for whom fear has made a home in their hearts, give them the emotional rest their souls desire.*

Reflection Questions

1. Have you ever been in conflict with someone, and seen him/her again once the conflict ended? How did you feel when you saw him/her?

2. Does the fear of seeing them again trick you into believing you have done something wrong or that you will enter another conflict?

3. Are you living at peace with everyone in your life (meaning you have done your best to make peace?) What can you do to try to establish peace with those people?

Thanksgiving is the Key to Eradicating Fear

"Do not be anxious about anything, but in every situation, by prayer and petition, with thanksgiving, present your requests to God"- Philippians 4:6.

I have known how to pray since I was a child. With a quick "Dear Lord" I'd summon God like a gumball machine, inserting my coin and waiting for the magic treat to land in my hand. I'd ask for whatever I wanted and expected God to deliver my every whim and desire like a genie in a bottle. But when I began an intimate relationship with Jesus at the age of eighteen, I didn't get everything I wanted. It was downright frustrating. Isn't that the purpose of communing with God?

As in any relationship, both parties involved must give to the other in order to make it successful. Although there are times when one must take and the other give, balance must be achieved or else the relationship becomes one-sided. In my relationship with God, I can give God nothing, as He has all He needs. The one thing I can give Him is my gratitude and thanks for all He does, even if it doesn't arrive the way or in the time frame I think it should.

Fear flees in the face of thanksgiving. When I am focused on being thankful, I don't have time to be afraid. Fear means I want to avoid a different outcome than the one God gives me. When I am thankful, I am content with whatever God gives, whenever He decides to give it.

Prayer: *Lord, do I approach you with thanksgiving, or with selfishness and greed? Help me to be thankful and content with whatever you decide in every situation.*

Reflection Questions

1. Do you approach God with contentment and thanksgiving?

2. How do you think thanksgiving is the key to eradicate fear?

3. Do you treat your relationships with a desire to give as much as you receive?

Discover your Purpose

Find Your Purpose

"This is what the LORD says: 'When seventy years are completed for Babylon, I will come to you and fulfill my good promise to bring you back to this place. For I know the plans I have for you,' declares the LORD, 'plans to prosper you and not to harm you, plans to give you hope and a future'" Jeremiah 29:11.

When I was in college, I prayed about what God wanted me to do with my life. After much prayer, Scripture study and consideration, I decided to go for my Master's degree in counseling. It would allow me to meet my desire to help others and put my spiritual gifts of wisdom and mercy to good use. I completed class after class, completely fulfilled in my decision. I had found my calling!

A friend at church was a licensed counselor. I asked if I could get some insight from her about the counseling field. When we sat down to meet, I asked her what my next steps were as I approached my internship and last classes. Furrowing her brow, she said plainly, "If you could do anything else, do it." I was shocked! Didn't she like her job? Didn't she want to see me succeed? She clarified and expressed her concerns about the future of the field and how Christian counseling was not the same as secular counseling. With smaller Christian counseling centers shutting down due to financial difficulties and lack of qualified counselors, she warned me about the lack of opportunities that awaited me at the other side of the university door. She grew concerned about the long hours and trying cases. She enjoyed her job, but she said it was tiring and took a special type of person. She ended the conversation challenging me to assess whether or not I was the type of person that could handle the demands of the job.

Looking back on that meeting, it would be easy for me to place blame on her, saying if it weren't for her, I'd be fulfilling my calling as a licensed counselor today. But I'm not doing that.

Because it was the best thing that ever happened to me.

If it were not for her boldness to help me analyze whether this was the right job for me, I would not be free to explore God's will for my life. In fact, if I had followed what I believed was my calling, you wouldn't be reading this book! Even though I did not become a licensed counselor, God still uses my heart for helping others and my spiritual gifts in my writing and speaking. I use my gift of wisdom to interpret Scriptures in a new way and my gift of teaching through writing and speaking about my various book topics.

Perhaps you know a woman who is struggling with figuring out the plan God has for them. They could feel intimidated because everyone else seems to have their lives figured out while they feel trapped and stuck in ambiguity. Simply because they have not found one specific job that is perfect for them does not mean God does not have a purpose for their lives.

God had a plan for His people, but it would not be completed for seventy years. God said this to encourage the people to faithfully obey His commands because after his purpose in Babylon was completed, He would bring them back to a more familiar land.

I can imagine this is a different plan than what His people expected. Exiled from their homeland, they were being transferred to a completely new place. Yet God was preparing them for something he had for them in the future.

God wants us to follow him above all else. But He also allows us the capacity to dream. We can envision how we think our lives should go, but those dreams need to align with God's will for us, for he is the only one who knows what the future holds for all of us.

Prayer: *Lord, help me discover my purpose through you.*

Reflection Questions

1. Did you have a plan for your life that didn't go the way you had hoped?

2. How did you react when your plans got derailed?

3. How can we not get mad at God but instead channel that anger into contentment that God has us in the palm of his hand?

A New Career

"Jesus called them, and immediately they left the boat and their father and followed Him"- Matthew 4:22.

Following the calling that is deep in your heart is not an easy task. I can remember the day I decided to leave the comfortability of everything I knew to venture into the starting of my company, Joyful Parties Boutique. I felt just as these disciples did. I heard the call. I stepped out in faith. I booked a flight to Miami for a two-week training in event decorating. Everyone thought I was crazy, including me. But I had the determination to see just how far my faith could take me. I know this is not always the case.

There are always so many excuses that can convince you to play it safe. I can imagine many possible excuses the disciples could have made when Jesus called them out to follow him.

"Sure Jesus, I'll get right on that. When I'm done paying my bills, when I'm done taking the fish to town, when I'm done selling them, when my boat is paid off and my debt is cleared." "Yeah, God, when this show is over, I will join you then, I promise." Or better yet "God, just let me follow you on Instagram or Facebook so we can just chat there. I'll text you whenever I'm free." We try to convince ourselves that it's OK to put God aside but really at the end of the day the world doesn't choose to put us in heaven or hell. Guess who does? God.

The Bible doesn't say that the disciples just added Jesus on Snapchat. It says that they left their jobs all at once to follow him. Who in their right mind does that? Walked off their jobs because someone is calling them to follow Him.

Today, I beckon you to listen closely to the call that is drawing you out of your comfort zone into the newfound career that God has for you. Do not allow excuses or fear to deter you from what's on the other side of your comfort zone. Why would you keep a dying bouquet of roses when our Father has a fresh new bouquet instead?

Since they decided to walk off the job and to follow Jesus, they changed the course of history. Jesus may not be calling you to quit your job, although He may, He is calling you to follow Him and what He placed inside of you. There could be a new career that's waiting to be explored that may change the world and change history. You are a world changer. But before you change the world, He's calling you to put your trust in Him. Have faith and it will create a whole new career.

Prayer: *Father, I thank you for calling me into the deep. I know greatness lives within me, therefore, I will trust you and I will allow every good gift inside of me to be used to change a world that you love. I will not fear, nor will I fret. But I will walk boldly into this new career that you are calling me to. In you I trust, Amen.*

Reflection Questions

1. Think about it do you have the faith to believe God if he asked you to follow him and leave your area of comfort?

2. Do you make God wait before you obey him when he asks you to do a hard thing?

3. What is God calling you to do that requires complete faith?

Rediscovering your Purpose

"Consider how far you have fallen! Repent and do the things you did at first. If you do not repent, I will come to you and remove your lampstand from its place"- Revelation 2:5.

S ometimes you may feel as if everything in your life is falling apart and has no meaning. You may not know where you are or what you are doing. Your mind is so empty. How did this happen? Maybe you felt like you couldn't see your way out of this state of melancholy. Life feels as if there is no light to guide you. Almost as if you are trapped in an eternal ominous world. In this very moment you should reevaluate your purpose.

Jesus threatens to remove the candlestick out of its place because they were not fulfilling its purpose. God hates waste. We are not to waste any gift or talent God has given us. In doing this you will lead yourself into sin and not to mention a waste of God's time. The next day is not promised so why would we waste precious days? There is so much value in this life so why waste it? If we think about it, none of us likes to have our time wasted especially by someone we love.

Nevertheless, God loved his kids enough to give them another opportunity to return to their first love: loving Him. Yes, God loved his children enough to want to be their best selves. Sometimes this may cause you to have to go back and rediscover your purpose and why He created you.

It is super easy for us as moms to fall out of place with God and into idol worship, whether it be putting people, places or things before God and everything He put inside of you to cultivate.

I challenge you to allow your light to shine for the world to see, weather at home, on the job or in your daily routines. Know that if you have fallen away and can't seem to see. He is waiting with loving arms to restore you.

Prayer: *Father, let me not waste the gifts you have given me. Instead, let me use all I have for your glory. Amen.*

Reflection Questions

1. What is the ultimate purpose of your life?

2. Be radically honest, what fears, and insecurities are holding you back from using your gifts God has given you to be your best self?

3. Are you willing to put in effort to rediscover your purpose?

What Are Spiritual Gifts?

"Now about the gifts of the Spirit, brothers and sisters, I do not want you to be uninformed." 1 Corinthians 12:1.

S o often I hear women trying to boost their self-esteem without identifying the root of the issue. One of the main issues surrounding self-esteem is the lack of purpose someone feels. As soon as women enter adulthood, they begin to ask themselves questions such as:

"Why am I here?"

"What should I do with my life?"

"What does my future hold?"

The church can be a great place to help women answer those questions. From the beginning of time, God has placed within each one of His children with a set of abilities that are wired according to their personalities. Everyone who has decided to embark on a daily journey in a deeper walk with God has received a specific set of gifts (called spiritual gifts) that are used to help people find their specific role within the body of Christ.

Part of being a disciple is becoming aware of what gifts God has given and using them to fulfill a person's ultimate purpose. Ephesians 2:10 says, "For we are God's handiwork created in Christ Jesus to do good works, which God prepared in advance for us to do." God has a plan for not only your life but in all women's lives as well. Their destinies are waiting to be discovered and they need you to help them discover it.

A spiritual gift is a God-given ability given by the Holy Spirit to followers of Jesus Christ that build others up into maturity in Christ.

Jesus said in John 14:12, "whoever believes in me will do the works that I am doing, and they will do even greater things than these, because I am going to the Father." Jesus goes on to explain to them how this will be possible, through the power of the Holy Spirit. But often times we don't experience ourselves doing the things Jesus did, let alone greater things than Jesus did. One of the reasons we don't understand spiritual gifts is because we don't understand how the Holy Spirit gifts and empowers us. Without the Holy Spirit we are nothing. We cannot use our gifts to further God's work in the kingdom without the Spirit's power. To neglect to understand our gifts is to neglect our purpose.

Prayer: *Lord, help me to understand the gifts God has given and therefore discover my purpose.*

Reflection Questions

1. How are spiritual gifts and purpose interrelated?

2. If you have not known that you have gifts, how does that make you feel? If you regularly use your gifts, how do you feel when you are using them?

3. What do you think Jesus means when He says, "We will do greater things than these?"

Embracing God's Mission

"When the LORD replied: 'Write down the revelation and make it plain on tablets so that a herald may run with it'" Habakkuk 2:2.

God calls us to a much larger mission than to come together on a Sunday service as individuals just to get a spiritual filling. As His people, we glorify Him when we use our gifts in a tangible way to serve the people in our churches and then as a collective body meet the needs of our communities. We connect when we serve each other.

The ways that we connect others to a community not only to meet their need for intimacy but also empower them to connect to others are the ripple effect we create. One person investing mentally, emotionally, and spiritually into others in the hopes they will then pay it forward. That's how Jesus ministered to His disciples and that's how fruit is produced. Not just any fruit, but good fruit, the fruit that lasts.

Christians need to ask themselves, "What's my story?" What experiences, circumstances or situations has God put me through that I can learn from and in turn edify the people God puts in my path? Your stories are not just random coincidences; they are opportunities to glorify God and bring the good news to a dying world.

To participate in other people's stories is to embrace God's greater mission, the one He writes for each of His children as they seek to know him and transform into his image. As church members embrace and understand the bigger mission of their role in the church body, they can help lead and guide everyone into a healthy discipleship relationship, each giving of themselves to achieve the desired result: spiritual growth.

Prayer: *Lord, help me discover and embrace the mission you have for my life.*

Discussion Questions

1. How is a person's story connected to the greater mission God has for his people?

2. What parts of your story do you think God can use for His glory?

3. How do you think God is going to use your story (even the parts that seem undesirable or useless to the Lord)? Pray and ask God to reveal His will for your story. Write down what He reveals on the lines on the opposite page.

Be in Community

We Are Called to Be Part of a Community

"Two are better than one, because they have a good return for their labor: If either of them falls down, one can help the other up. But pity anyone who falls and has no one to help them up" Ecclesiastes 4:9.

This idea of community is repeated throughout the entire Bible from Genesis to Revelation and is even honored and encouraged. God Himself does not exist as one Supreme Being, but chooses to exist in three persons: Father, Son, and Holy Spirit. Each part of the Trinity achieves equality with God yet has different distinct roles. All contribute together to make one God.

God owes us nothing, needs nothing, yet He chose to create us for the joy of fellowship with us. Proverbs 27:17 compares, "As iron sharpens iron, so one person sharpens another." As I envision this verse, I imagine two iron rods rubbing together. As the two rub together, each rod gives a little of itself away in order for the other to sharpen itself. In the same way, the above verse talks about how strong we can be if we are together. Surrounding ourselves with other brothers and sisters in Christ is vital, therefore, we can do the work of the Kingdom more speedily and have a more lasting impact.

The Acts church came together out of necessity. They came together not only to worship, but to marvel in Jesus' miraculous death and resurrection.

They gave up everything, including their safety and security, to meet together.

If the Acts Church understood the need for regularly worshipping together, why shouldn't we?

Prayer: *Lord, help me to find other Christians who will partner with me in community so we can be stronger together, doing work for the Kingdom for you here on earth.*

Discussion Questions

1. Why does surrounding ourselves with other Christians make us stronger?

2. Why do you think we can accomplish more work for the Kingdom when we do it together in community?

3. Who can you partner with to help you do the work of the Kingdom? Write down their names on the lines and then prayerfully ask them for their partnership.

Day Thirty-Three

Who Holds Your Hands Up?

When Moses' hands grew tired, they took a stone and put it under him and he sat on it. Aaron and Hur held his hands up--one on one side, one on the other--so that his hands remained steady till sunset- Exodus 17:12.

One morning as I greeted people coming into my church, I watched horrifically as a man who was having severe back pain hobble into the foyer, too bent over to stand upright. He came to seek healing from the Lord. I knew I needed to do something, but what? I put his arm around his shoulder and I, along with another woman, became his hands and feet as we walked with the man to the front vacant seat in the sanctuary. His physical illness incapacitated him, rendering him unable to walk for himself. However, after some elders laid hands and prayed for him, he was able to walk upright! I had witnessed a miracle.

Although this man was the exception, I have prayed for many people in our church, but their requests for a miracle were never answered. This, along with mass shootings as an almost daily occurrence in our world and mental illness ravaging the Church, makes it hard to fight in these spiritual battles, especially when it feels like the enemy's arrows are too numerous to defeat.

When I get weary, I need mature Christians who are willing to figuratively (and maybe literally) lift my arms up when I am too weary to keep them up.

Who holds up your hands?

Do you have sisters and brothers in Christ who are willing to encourage you when you are down and challenge you because they care enough about you to make you better?

Prayer: *Lord, give us people within the body of Christ that hold up our hands when we are weary. Amen.*

Reflection Questions

1. Why do you think it is important for you to be in community with those who can help you in your Christian walk?

2. Who has God placed in your path to lift up your hands when you are weary?

3. Are these people most similar or most dissimilar to you? Why do you think it is important to be with people dissimilar to you?

"I Get by With A Little Help from My Friends"

"As iron sharpens iron, so one man sharpens another"- Proverbs 27:17.

O ne of my favorite television programs as a kid is *The Wonder Years*, a show about an eleven-year old boy (played by Fred Savage) muddling through the exciting yet unchartered waters of puberty. Every week I would watch as Kevin Arnold stumbled through Junior High School with his friend Paul Pfeiffer and fawned over his crush and next- door neighbor Winnie Cooper. The show was about a nuclear family trying to survive the tumultuous decade of free love, the sexual revolution and new advancements both in space and in the world. Each week, viewers listened as Joe Cocker crooned the show's theme, the cover of the Beatles song "I Get by with a Little Help from My Friends." There was comfort in knowing that Kevin had his faithful friend Paul, his love Winnie and his family to help him through life's trials.

It's like this in our spiritual lives, too. God has placed us with brothers and sisters in Christ who are there to support, encourage and keep us accountable so that we can grow in our walks. The intention is that no matter how difficult the trials we are going through right now, we do not have to walk alone. Sometimes we follow in the footsteps of mature Christians, placing ourselves in each print so we don't lose our way. Other times we need to lead the less mature Christian so that they don't stray and know which way to go.

But so often we try to do the Christian life alone. We choose a random path, walking and getting lost with no real direction or end goal in sight. It is important we have others in our lives who are gifted differently than us so that we can sharpen one another in an effort to become more like Christ.

Prayer: *Lord, help me to find the right type of people that can support, encourage and keep me accountable when I needed it the most. Amen.*

Reflection Questions

1. Do you have people in your life who lead you and that you lead in return?

2. Who has God placed in your life to help you through life's journey?

3. Why do you think it is important to stay in community with each other?

Life is Better When We Do It Together

"For where two or three gather in my name, there am I with them"- Matthew 18:20.

The other night, my daughter and I enjoyed the warm night air as we walked around the track at our local football field. As we walked, my daughter kept stopping, complaining of boredom and a sudden onset of stomach cramps. Frustrated, I walked ahead of her, determined to get in a much-needed cardio workout. Suddenly, I felt the Lord whisper in my ear:

Isn't the point of this walk to enjoy some quality time with your daughter?

I stopped abruptly, turned 180 degrees in the opposite direction, and caught up to my daughter. For one night, it didn't matter how many calories I burned or how much exercise I needed. That moment, I dropped my agenda and enjoyed walking and talking with my daughter.

If I'm honest it is like this in every area of my life, including my spiritual life.

I often approach my prayer time with my agenda of prayer requests, ready to check it off my mental to- do list and eager to get on with my day. But God wants more from us than just a laundry list of wishes to grant like he's some genie in a bottle. He wants me. Not just part of me, but all of me. He doesn't just want me to walk in isolation in my spiritual journey. He wants me to partner with others.

Sometimes He wants me to catch up to those struggling in their walks, willing to trade my agenda for His. Other times He wants me to sprint to catch up to those further on in the distance to catch up with those who will push me to grow in my walk. We were never meant to walk this journey alone. Life is so much better when I do it with others.

Prayer: *Lord, help me partner with others and walk along our spiritual journey together.*

Discussion Questions

1. Has there been a time when you treated your relationship with Jesus like a to-do list? How do you think that affects your intimacy with God?

2. Are there times when you treat your relationships with others like to-do lists? How does that affect your relationships with them?

3. Do you think God honors the time I spend investing in others? How so?

Day Thirty-Six

Social Media and a Need for Community

"Jesus went to solitary places to pray"- Mark 1:35.

C hurch is often the primary way Christians meet to worship and connect. But saying "Hi" on a Sunday morning is not enough to meet a deeper need for intimacy. You need a place where you can share your feelings and meet your needs for community and connection. We were never made to go this spiritual journey alone. But so often we pray, worship and read our Bibles without any support network to correct, train and cultivate maturity within us.

Churches are more than just a chance to gain more knowledge; it's a chance to apply that knowledge to everyday life while meeting a deep need for intimacy and connection with other like- minded individuals.

We all need (and want) to belong. It is in our DNA. We can fool ourselves into thinking we can journey through life on our own. Our need for human connection and contact can never be met in a solo effort. Just as the disciples traveled in twos, we also are called to grow in our faith with our brothers and sisters in Christ.

Adam and Eve broke fellowship with their father through their choice to disobey Him. But they also missed out on something else. Through severing their fellowship with God, they cut off the gift of continual communion with Him.

Jesus, during his time on earth, knew in order to minister effectively, He would have to constantly reestablish the deep connection that met His true needs for intimacy. This is so He would be in continual communion with God. This is why after a long day of ministry, Jesus often went to solitary places to pray (Mark 1:35, Matthew 14:23, Luke 6:12.)

Because we live in a broken world, one Sunday morning service does not fully satisfy our needs for connection. We need to reestablish connection and communion with the Father regularly. This is why small groups meet those needs for fellowship and community.

Social media has tried to replace the church by creating an online forum where people can speak their minds on anything (and sometimes tear others down in the process). Studies show that places like Facebook, instead of meeting the need for connection and community, leaves you more starved for real connection than ever before. Because the church is not meeting that need, you may begin to look elsewhere.

Some things in life are only to be shared with a few mature people, while other things can be shared with a larger group. Small groups (ideally 4-5 members) provide the forum you need to share your most intimate thoughts and feelings without the risk of public humiliation.

Churches meet the need for connection and intimacy in a way social media never can. The world will try to provide you with a counterfeit version of real community through social media. As you seek to meet your need for connection, social media will try to meet it, but it will fall short. As you walk the journey of spiritual growth together, your need for the world's validation and worth will lessen.

Prayer: *Lord, let me not substitute social media as a counterfeit source of community. Instead, let me spend time with the people whom you have placed in my life.*

Reflection Questions

1. How do you think social media is a counterfeit version of real community?

2. How can small groups help meet your need for connection and community?

3. Why did Jesus choose to spend most of his time with His disciples?

Kill Condemnation

I'm Not Perfect but I Am Perfectly Made

"For God did not send his Son into the world to condemn the world, but to save the world through him"- John 3:17.

We mothers tend to beat ourselves up because we want to be perfect to the people who look up to us. There were many times I felt ashamed of a lot of the choices I made. Condemnation tends to creep in often because we love to take on a superhero mindset, always striving to come to the rescue with all the answers. Being praised for it doesn't help us in this department. God had already sent His son to die for us and purify our mistakes. He knew condemnation would bring stagnation into our lives, and being stagnated is not a place we need to be.

Sometimes we look at other people and their lives and wish that somehow, we could measure up to their achievements. It's not necessarily that we want to be exactly like them, but we may feel like we want to have some great achievements, too. Condemning thoughts flood our mind with everything that we are not. I have talked to enough women to know I am not the only one who is hard on herself. Quick to point a finger inward and prone to believe our condemning thoughts are coming from God himself. Perhaps you have heard this before:

I'm not Mom enough. I am too much of the wrong things and not the right things.

I can't possibly step out in ways that God has given me.

Everyone will see my faults and weaknesses.

Lies, lies, lies.

God knows we aren't perfect. We don't have to be perfect to be His children.

He takes each weakness and flaw and He uses it for His glory. He is able to show His power in the changes He makes in your life so every time you feel *less than* know that you serve a God that is *greater than* all things. He takes broken things and makes them beautiful. Tell condemnation not to take root in your heart.

Prayer: *Daddy, you are the ultimate perfection. You make all things beautiful and perfect in your own way. I am your creation and I am perfectly made in your likeness and image. Lord, I thank you for your ultimate sacrifice and I will not allow condemnation to take root in my heart. Amen.*

Reflection Questions

1. Examine some of the things that cause you to stumble that are lies that come for condemnation.

2. What are some triggers that causes condemnation to enter into your life?

3. Pick 2 scripture and write them down to memorize when negative thoughts about you begin to raise up in your life.

I Am Who He Says I Am

"Therefore, there is now no condemnation for those who are in Christ Jesus"-
Romans 8:1.

D o you really know who you are? Are you sure? What (or who) gives
you identity? There are many people who judge you are based on your
past decisions, whether good or bad. People believe you are what you
do. You are not who people say you are but you are who your creator made you
to be. I've made a lot of mistakes in my life, trust me, but none of them make me
who I am. Nor does God condemn me. This is something that we do to ourselves.

Condemnation comes from Satan and aims to destroy. On the contrary, the
conviction we experience is Godly sorrow and prompts change. God loves you
with an everlasting love. Don't be condemned for you are a generation changer.
You've been called to change your generation. You are not just lamb, but a lion.
Satan tries to convince us he's a lion and he may come in like one, but he is not a
lion he's a liar! You may have made many mistakes but don't feel condemned
because God didn't give us condemnation, but at times he will convict us and
there is nothing wrong with that. The word of God says that we are fearfully and
wonderfully made. We are His choice stone, his gem. We are victorious through
Him and Him only. You are who God says you are and his word shall never
return unto Him void. Repent and forgive yourself of anything that you have
done so you may move forward and do all He calls you to do. Remember
condemnation shouts your past but conviction shouts the blood of Jesus shall
wash away all sins!

Prayer: *Lord, we position ourselves to receive You daily. We know that the word
will work on those who believe. I believe every word you said about me.*

*I know I have done wrong, but you said if I confess my sins you are faithful and
just to forgive me. Help me get closer to you and not be condemned. I love you,
Father, and ask you to keep teaching me.*

In your sovereign name I prayer. Amen.

Reflection Questions

1. Describe what you thought or felt in your moment of shame and how did you form your view of yourself?

2. Who holds your identity? Has your past mistake caused you to question who you are?

3. Do you live like Romans 8:1 is true? How would truly believing this transform your life?

Build Each Other Up

Likewise, the tongue is a small part of the body, but it makes great boasts. Consider what a great forest is set on fire by a small spark. The tongue also is a fire, a world of evil among the parts of the body. It corrupts the whole body, sets the whole course of one's life on fire, and is itself set on fire by hell- James 3:5-6.

Changes are happening over the past few months at my church, and with those changes the fiery darts from the enemy are flying, poised to hit everyone in their way. But they aren't literal darts, of course. The darts were coming out of the mouths of seemingly spiritual Christians who weren't happy with the church's current situation. Instead of dealing with it directly, speaking to the parties responsible for the changes, they instead talked to each other, letting their gossip spread from one innocent person to another. Even with the best intentions, people not only destroy their relationships with each other but also with God.

There is a reason God gifted us with two ears and one mouth. We were created to do twice as much listening as we are talking! I know what it is like to be talked about behind my back, and it's not fun. It hurts, and it damages my reputation not only as a woman but also has a Christian.

If I'm honest, though, there is a small part of me that likes to hear (and dispense) gossip. Part of me likes to tear others down because in a twisted way, it builds me up. But it is only a temporal pleasure that fills the void in my heart due to a lack of intimacy with God. When I am in fellowship with God, I don't thrive off of other's failures. But when I am out of fellowship with Him, I look for any morsel of gossip to devour, quickly to spit put to the first willing ear.

Before you open your mouth to gossip, ask yourself the following questions:

- Would I be saying this if the person was standing next to me?

- Is what I'm saying a biblical response to my current circumstances?

- Have I checked my heart before I say this to others?

Gossip is an outward symptom of an inward heart issue. Gossip flows out of a heart that is chocked full of criticism, selfishness and greed, looking only to its own interests rather than the interests of others. The permanent way to fix my heart and zip my lips is to run to God with my issues, pouring my heart out to Him instead of complaining to others. When I handle my feelings in a biblical way, I'm way less likely to indulge in the pleasure gossip provides.

Prayer: *Lord, help me not to tear others down in order to build each other up. If I do hear gossip, help me not to spread it to others. Most importantly, help me to connect with you so that gossip will lose its appeal. Amen.*

Reflection Questions

1. Where are you in your relationship with God? Are you in a good spot in your relationship with God so that you are not tempted to gossip?

2. Have you gossiped about someone? Take a moment to make amends with that person. Contact him/her and apologize for your sin.

3. Have you heard gossip about someone? What can you do to prevent spreading gossip about others?

Celebrate the Victories

Celebrate the Everyday Adventures in Life

"All this is for your benefit, so that the grace that is reaching more and more people may cause thanksgiving to overflow to the glory of God"-2 Corinthians 4:15.

In the movie *Up*, Carl and his wife spend the first years of their lives planning for the grand adventure: living in a house on a remote place in Mexico. Ellie creates a scrapbook where she adds pictures of "all the things she's going to do." As life often does, house repairs, car repairs and unexpected circumstances keep them from saving the money for them to reach their destination. Before they know it, life has passed them by and Ellie, now an old woman, gives the scrapbook to Carl to fill with his life's adventures. He opens the scrapbook to find not a bunch of empty pages because of life preventing them from experiencing Ellie's dream destination, but of the small moments of life, the ones we look back on when we are old and realize they are what made life an adventure.

Thanksgiving is a time for friends, family and spending time together. It's also a time on Facebook when people post a thirty- day thanksgiving challenge where people post what they are grateful for on their statuses, in the hopes it will flood people's feeds with positivity and gratitude rather than negativity and selfishness. While I think this is a wonderful idea, I wonder why we don't take each day to find the moments we are most grateful for. Why would we wait for one month (or day) of the year to express gratitude? Life is short.

No one knows when those grand adventure moments will end for us or for our loved ones.

Let's shift our attitudes from one day of thankfulness to being grateful every day for what God has given us. Starting this week, start a journal. For the next thirty days, recall the daily moments that make our lives an adventure. It could be anything: eating ice cream with your kids, playing catch with your dog, holding hands with your significant others.

Instead of posting it on Facebook for just one month (although you can feel free to do that if you choose), get a bulletin board and take pictures of those moments and tack them onto your board.

Why only take one day to be thankful when you can be grateful every day? Why not take every day to be thankful for the little adventures in life?

Prayer: *Lord, help me to be grateful every day for the little moments that make life wonderful.*

Reflection Questions

1. Do you think it will be easy for you to record the moments that make life adventurous?

2. What prevents you from being grateful every day?

3. How do you think shifting your perspective to one of gratitude will help your spiritual life?

Day Forty-One

Don't Forget to Celebrate

"Celebrate all day, every day."-Philippians 4:4

One Sunday at church, my husband preached about the celebration as an important part of a Christian's life. He said it was a discipline that, when practiced, can help develop us into mature Christians. At that point, he grabbed the microphone from the pulpit and said, "What is God doing in your life? Let's share and celebrate together." He waited for several minutes, and as he waited, he received one thing:

Silence.

People were hesitant to share because the culture of the church emphasized silence and listening rather than talking and noise. Church should not only be a place for prayer and soul searching but a place to celebrate the ways God is speaking and moving in our lives.

If I'm honest, I have difficulty celebrating the good things in life. My tendency is to focus on the negatives instead of the positives, telling people what God *isn't* doing rather what He *is* doing.

Do you celebrate with others when God does something good in your life? If we are not celebrating others' accomplishments, how can we breathe life into the body of Christ?

The church is a place to bear each other's burdens and allow God to work deep within our souls. But it should also be a place where we as brothers and sisters celebrate the good things God is doing as well. Life is full of miracles. God is always with us and at work in our lives.
If you challenged yourself to write down every time you saw God working in your life, you could fill an entire notebook. It's important to celebrate all of the ways (big and small) that God revealed Himself to you or the people you know.

Here are three ways you can celebrate at your next church service:

Share–Is there someone (or a group of people) at your church with whom you can share your blessings and accomplishments?

Allow them to have you over for dinner or take you out to celebrate. Make time in your weekly service to allow congregation members to share what God is doing in their lives. It will encourage those going through a difficult time and help them to become more aware of the ways in which God is working.

Model-In the same way others celebrate with you, spend some time celebrating with others. To do this, you must be aware of what is going on with the people within your congregation. Ask others how their life is going. Remember what they said and follow up with them the following week. Show you care and people will open up to you.

Pray-Ask the people in your congregation for specific prayer requests and pray diligently for those requests. When a prayer gets answered, reciprocate by sending a gift or card or take them out to celebrate how God is moving.

Church can be a boring place, or it can be a place where we as God's children can celebrate all the good things God is doing, even when under difficult circumstances. Will you choose to celebrate with your brothers and sisters in Christ?

Prayer: *Help me take little moments every day and celebrate what you are doing in our lives.*

Discussion Questions
1. Do you celebrate the everyday moments where God is present?

2. If the answer to the above question is no, why do you find it difficult?

3. How do you think you can incorporate celebration into your life?

Fulfilled Promises

"Blessed is she who has believed that the Lord would fulfill his promises"-Luke 1:45.

Have you ever been in a situation where you did not have anything else left to hold on to besides the word of God?

My friend packed up her car, with a suitcase, an acceptance letter from a prestigious school in the Big Apple and a bucket filled with hope. Her parents passed away when she was a little girl, so she only lived with her sister at the time. When she received the acceptance letter from school, she knew it was God's plan for her life. With God's direction, she was able to drive five hours away from home into a new place. She did not know where she was going to stay, eat or work. She only knew that God was directing her into a new journey.

When she arrived in New York City with her two kids, the Lord led her to a church where she received her next instructions. She did not know why this church was calling her, but she refrained from asking too many questions and proceeded. There she sat at church with her two kids in an unfamiliar place without any additional family support. As she headed towards the exit, a church member grabbed her hand asking her where she was from. The same sister offered her a place to stay that same night until she was ready to get back on her two feet.

Two years in New York City she was able to complete school, obtain her own apartment, begin her own business and serve God throughout her journey. It was then when she was able to truly thank God and celebrate in victory. She was willing to step outside of her comfort zone and fully devote herself to God's promise.

Her faith took her places that she never imagined. Most importantly, throughout her journey of moving away from home she was able to uncover her identity. Because she was able to hold onto the promise of God, she was blessed.

I invite you to be take a piece of this courageous story and apply it to your journey. Understand that the promise that God has for you is bigger than fear. There is much more waiting for you on the other side. Be willing to act on the radical faith that is already within you and press towards God's promise over your life. The more you trust God, the more space He will have to work within you and that is where the blessing comes from.

Prayer: *Heavenly Father, thank you for giving me the strength to press towards your promises. You see the beginning and the end to everything oh Lord, and because of that I trust you more than I trust myself.*

Reflection Questions

1. List 3 promises that have yet to be manifested that you are holding onto with all your strength?

2. Ask yourself why do you fear when you don't see the manifestation of Gods promises over your life right away?

3. In your own words write down a prayer expressing gratitude for promises God has already kept.

Fill the Void

God's Gift to Man

"I know that there is nothing better for the people than to be happy and to do good while they live. That each of them may eat and drink and find satisfaction in all their toil- this is the gift of God"- Ecclesiastes 3:12-13.

About 13 years ago, I was suffering from a disease doctors couldn't diagnose. It caused me to become very tired and would give me abdominal pain as if I was having another child. The pain was unbearable! It felt like a million bees were swarming around in my belly and stinging me. When I went to the doctor, he explained to me that this was something that has become very common to people who were overworked and or stressed. He asked me something very strange: "Are you resting? Are you stressed Mrs. Langhorn?" When I didn't reply he looked at me with a blank stare. He replied, "Our stomachs and intestines are connected and have their own nervous system, called the enteric nervous system. These nerves respond to the same stress hormones and neurotransmitters that our brains do, this may cause intestinal inflammation and yes it was caused by stress." I looked at him flabbergasted. I didn't realize that taking care of the body was vital in more ways than I knew. That the dis -ease I was putting my body through was causing diseases to take residence. That stress and working all the time was causing my stomach to light up on fire. I suddenly realized that if I didn't slow down and take better care of myself, I wouldn't be able to support my own kids. Of course, I began to focus on how to take better care of myself and keep myself balanced.

Moms and caregivers all over the world may be at a higher risk of developing what I call "Workabetes." Although it is not a real disease, Workabetes has the same chemical composition as diabetes.

Just as diabetes results when a chemical imbalance occurs in the body from too much sugar, Workabetes occurs when there is an imbalance of work and leisure in a person's life. In order to maintain physical, mental, emotional and spiritual health, we must schedule adequate personal time.

I was in my own stage of Workabetes that I needed to reverse. We all can find ourselves suffering from something like this and, if gone unchecked, can cause spiritual and mental sickness as well. We serve a God who heals us from our pain. God wants each of us to keep going when we need to work, He also gives us strength to take time to relax and move past our restlessness. Even when we're going through a heavy season of work, we must remember we are going through it and that we don't have to stay in each adversity we are facing.

God ultimate desire is for us to be happy, whole, nothing missing, nothing lacking. He desires us to live in his fullness of joy. I have learned how to slow down and enjoy everything God has gifted me. Ever since I have put this into practice, I am healed! Those stomach pains have completely disappeared. Thank you Jesus!

Prayer: *Father help me not to be so busy that I forget to be happy. Thank you for revealing that it is your true desire that I prosper even as my soul prospers. Today I will learn how to dance, sing and enjoy life finding balance between work and play.*

Reflection Questions

1. What are some things that are stressing you that needs to be eliminated out of your life?

2. List 5 changes you need to make to better your health and your level of Joy?

3. Is over working something you struggle with? If so, how can you balance it out with some form of enjoyable activity that is relaxing and stress free?

Day Forty-Four
Soul Searching

"Make a careful exploration of who you are and the work you have been given, and then sink yourself into that. Don't be impressed with yourself. Don't compare yourself with others. Each of you must take responsibility for doing the creative best you can with your own life"- Galatians 6:4-5.

I finally figured out we all must make an effort to find out who God intended us to be when He formed us. We are all to seek God's blueprint for our lives. I am constantly searching through the Word of God to help me find prototypes and models that are laid out through Scripture. As the Scripture above instructs, we are not to concern ourselves with how the next person lives, to the point where we become envious or compete with them because as Psalms 139:14 already declares, "I am fearfully and wonderfully made."

Sometimes I look back to when my children were very little. I spent most of my time caring for them. Although many memorable moments were formed throughout the day, I felt overwhelmed at the end of each one. One night, I tucked my youngest into bed.

"Mommy can you read to me?" she cried with her round puppy dog eyes. I sighed with reluctance and began to read from the Children's Bible. As I read, I thought to myself, *Is this it?*

Is this what life has for me?

Changing diapers, wiping noses, cleaning up and telling bedtime stories? There's got to be more.

After all of my children were fast asleep, I turned on the TV and watched Grey's Anatomy.

This became a nightly routine. With each episode, I envied the lives of the characters. They seemed to live such adventurous lives that made my own life seem dull.

I realized that my reality should have never been measured up to what I perceived in someone else's life. Grey's Anatomy was just a TV show.

What was I thinking? The fact was I learned something from Dr. Grey. Dr. Grey was constantly trying to find her place in life just as I was, not knowing that all the pieces to the puzzles were right in front of her. Everything she was doing led her closer to purpose.

The Holy Spirit places pointers here and there for us as we grow. You need to trace your steps as far back as you can recall. Seek out what special things have stood out to you in your life. What problems did you seek to solve? You must soul search and you will find purpose crying out to you. You may begin now by asking the help of the Holy Spirit in this prayer.

Prayer: *Dear Lord, reveal your purpose for my life to me. Amen.*

Reflection Questions

1. What are some things that bring me personal fulfillment?

2. Have I adequately examined those things that I consider to be basic and essential to my life?

3. What roles have I allowed God to have in the planning of my life?

Thank God I Found Out (T.G.I.F.O)

"No temptation has overtaken you except what is common to mankind. And God is faithful; he will not let you be tempted beyond what you can bear. But when you are tempted, he will also provide a way out so that you can endure it"- 1 Corinthians 10:31.

I'd often shop at Walmart. I get googly eyes upon entering this place. I get ecstatic upon looking at the vast aisles of clothing, food, and makeup. With a large family, this store is a gold mine. Here's the problem: my husband often puts me on a budget and if anyone knows me, you know I hate budgets. It's really not the budget that I hate, it's the temptation to overspend. Yes, God is still delivering me from being a shopaholic. When I get in the store I have to try and stay within my budget, but everything is so intriguing. Overspending is one of my greatest temptations, yet God said He will not allow me to be tempted more than I can bear. He will always provide a way of escape and He has been teaching me self-control. You may not have the same exact temptation, but you may be facing some form of temptation. We have to make- up our minds to run from whatever may cause us to trip. I'm so glad I found out He has made a way of escape for me it's a fruit of the spirit called self-control.

Temptation is real! We face temptation every single day and each of our temptations are different. But we all have one thing in common: a God who provides a way out for each and every one of us. As long as we choose to believe in God, then He has a way out of every trial.

You will make it through if you trust his word. This I am sure of let's pray.

Prayer: *Thank you, Father, for you have taught us that no weapon formed against us shall prosper. You have given us strength and a way of escape. We appreciate you for helping us through when we can't help ourselves. Lord God, we thank you for your time and we ask you to keep giving us strength as we go through. Amen.*

Reflection Questions

1. List a few things that cause you to be tempted to do what is damaging to you?

2. Examine what triggers that follow this behavior and find way to counter act it with the word of God.

3. Now that you know that there is no temptation that God is not faithful enough to keep you from, how can you react to temptation when it comes to you?

I Am Not Alone

"The Lord is close to the brokenhearted and saves those who are crushed in spirit"-Psalm 34:18.

I love the book of Psalms because I identify with David. David was a man after God's own heart which means his heart had to be pretty big. But the bigger the heart, the greater the pain when it's broken. David would often cry to God, "Turn to me and be gracious to me for I am lonely and afflicted." We have all been there one time or another in our lives.

I have such a big heart for animals. I remember my dog, Diamond. She was a 100-pound black and brown Rottweiler that took pleasure in loving me back to life when I was down. She would often follow me around the house, never asking for anything but yearning for my company. One day I decided to take her for a walk outside. Noticing my shoe was untied, I bent down to fix it. As soon as I let go of her leash, her attention shifted to a squirrel a little far off. She dashed immediately for the squirrel and ran right into the middle of the street into oncoming traffic. The next thing I heard was the awful sound of the impact. A black jeep had hit her and dragged her body to the driveway where I was standing. My heart was crushed as I stood there in complete shock. Her chest rose slowly for the last time as her eyes fluttered shut. I ran to the stoop and cried. My brother-in-law ran out to Diamond with a blanket. He wrapped her up and carried her lifeless body into our backyard. Her blood seeped into the brick wall that divided my house from the next. And the enemy purposely wanted me to see it. The tears began to pour down my cheeks. I cried to God, "Why?" Trying to make sense of what just happened, all of a sudden it began to rain and just as quick as the enemy tried to taunt me with grief, God stepped in and the blood that was on the walls washed down. Suddenly I realized that I was not alone. God heard my cries and was washing away my tears.

This was one time out of many that I felt God so close to me.

I've found that it's in our hardest test and trials in life our loving father draws the closet to us. We may not feel it because of the pain but if you look past your pain you will find him right there. Delivering you from all hurt and brokenness.

Trust God to heal you as you meditate on what the Bible says about his love for you. Know that his mercies are new every single morning and He will be with you until the very end of the age. Utter these words in prayer with me.

Prayer: *Lord Jesus, teach me to rest in your love and your presence today and always. Even in the hardest time in life. Show me your love as I draw close to you because I know you are an ever-present help in time of need. Amen.*

Reflection Questions

1. When have you felt closest to God? What brought you there?

2. How can you use your heart break or disappointment to allow you to grow spiritual maturity in your relationship with God?

3. Think back to a time you were at your lowest did you look for God and what will you do differently now when you feel at your lowest in spirit?

The New Standard of Perfection

"Then the LORD *God formed a man from the dust of the ground and breathed into his nostrils the breath of life, and the man became a living being"*- Genesis 2:7.

"I didn't get perfect attendance," my daughter said as she hopped off the school bus.

She worked so hard all year, dodging every merciless flu bug just so she could stand in front of her classmates on the last day of school and wave her attendance certificate proudly for all to see. In my haste, I erroneously picked her up early from school one day, tarnishing her otherwise spotless record. I picked up the phone and furiously punched the numbers on the keypad. Speaking to the school secretary, she confirmed that she had indeed not received perfect attendance.

A myriad of self- debasing thoughts ran through my head. I had failed my daughter. Perhaps if I had waited one extra hour that day, I would not have robbed her of the distinct honor of having her teachers and peers acknowledge her achievement.

Before I could continue throwing myself a pity party, a thought flooded my head:

Why do you care if your daughter is seen as perfect?

The Lord, in His gentleness, was speaking to my heart. He reminded me of all the times I had come close to winning an award in school but fell short.

Every empty preschool sticker chart telling my friends how good I was, every bedroom shelf devoid of trophies every other child had received, every book contract that I hadn't signed, all screamed in my head:

You are unloved.

You are unworthy.

You are not good enough.

As I put the phone down in a huff and looked at my daughter, I saw a look of sadness overtake her face. My normally joyful child was preoccupied with her own thoughts of unworthiness. Then it dawned on me. She had not been working so hard all year for *her*; she had been working all year for *me*.

I was living vicariously through my daughter in a desperate attempt to fill her shelf with awards in order to fill the insecurities in my own heart. Although unspoken, I proclaimed the message that worthiness equals performance. The true failure had not come in falling short of the world's standard of perfection. The failure had come from falling short of God's standard of perfection.

God calls me to His standard of perfection, not one that boasts of neatly framed certificates on the wall but one that can candidly look in the mirror and accept myself for who I am, imperfections and all. A standard that can hug my daughter despite her imperfection and softly whisper, "you're perfect to me." A standard that reminds me that I am loved for who I *am* not for what I *do*.

You are loved for who you are, not for what you do, as difficult as it is for you to believe. The road to adopting this new standard will not be easy. There will be moments when you're tempted to lean on the world's standard of perfection once again, only to fall on your knees begging God for His unflinching grace. You'll want to base your worth and value on the insecurity of achievements, not in the security of the Savior's love.

When that happens, God will remind you of His standard of perfection:

You are loved.

You are worthy.

You are enough.

Prayer: *Help me not to live vicariously through my children. Help me to know my worth is found only in you, not in my accomplishments.*

Reflection Questions

1. Is it difficult for you to believe God loves you for who you are, not for what you do? Why or why not?

2. Are there people in your life that have made you believe you are worthy only for what you do?

3. How does God's love differ from the love you have experienced from others?

Revealing Every Part of Me to Appreciate God's Glory

"And we all, who with unveiled faces contemplate the Lord's glory, are being transformed into his image with ever-increasing glory, which comes from the Lord, who is the Spirit."- 2 Corinthians 3:18.

For many years as a Christian, I had a Sunday morning routine. I'd carefully lay out my clothes the night before. In the morning, I'd apply my makeup with precision, making sure not to make a mistake. I'd curl my hair into even ringlets, pulling it back into a symmetrical ponytail or bun. When I was done, I'd examine myself in the mirror, smoothing out wrinkles until everything was perfect. I'd walk into church pretending I was perfect, and from the outside appearance, and everyone's perceptions) I was.

But inwardly I was a mess.

Struggling in my spiritual life and not having (or desiring) to have a quiet time with the Lord in several months, on the outside I looked like everyone else, but on the inside, I was nothing but a hypocrite.

Have you ever felt like a hypocrite in your spiritual life? When all eyes are on you, do you pretend to have it all together, or do you fully embrace who you are, even the parts of you that seem undesirable?

In order to have a real relationship with God, I need to remove the makeup, wash my face and take down my hair so it flows freely. God knows who I am on the inside, warts and all. It is when I come to Him just as I am is when I truly meet with my Savior.

Then I can appreciate who God is in all His glory and God can fully appreciate me in all my glory too.

Prayer: *Lord, help me to be the real me to others. Help me avoid the temptation of covering up the undesirable parts of myself but rather embrace who I truly am so I (and others) can love the real me.*

Reflection Questions

1. Do you tend to cover up the parts of yourself you feel are undesirable? (Ex. your weight, your skin imperfections, etc.)

2. How does it make you feel to know God loves you just the way you are?

3. Does it cause you anxiety to reveal all of yourself to God and others? Or do you feel a sense of freedom?

Day Forty-Nine

Wasting Time with Jesus

"But Martha was distracted with all her preparations; and she came up to Him and said, 'Lord, do you not care that my sister has left me to do all the serving alone? Then tell her to help me.' But the Lord answered and said to her, 'Martha, Martha, you are worried and bothered about so many things; but only one thing is necessary, for Mary has chosen the good part, which shall not be taken away from her'" Luke 10:40-42 (NIV).

As I sat down in my favorite chair with my favorite morning beverage, I opened my Bible to the last place I read and began to read. Soon, however, my mind wandered to my daily to do list:

I have to put in the extra load of wash when this load is done.

I have to drop off my daughter's Science project to school.

I have to make sure my notes are prepared for work tomorrow.

My stomach turned as I tried to concentrate on the day's Bible passage. But the guilt I felt for not giving my whole heart and mind to my devotions made me shut my bible in disgust. I didn't want to admit it, but I actually felt guilty for spending time with the Lord, because I felt I was wasting precious time, I needed to dedicate to the other tasks demanding my time. Determined to meet with the Lord, I opened my Bible once again and came across this passage about Mary and Martha.

Like Martha, I often become so distracted for what I have to do *for* Jesus that I forget to spend time *with* Jesus. In the worries of the day, it's easy to get caught up in the next task to check off our lists.

It pleases Jesus when we dedicate our time using our gifts to serve Him and edify our brothers and sisters in Christ.

Prayer: *Daddy, help us to forsake our to- do lists for the sake of being with you. Amen.*

Discussion Questions

1. Do you focus more on what you have done for Jesus rather than spending time with Him?

2. How can you shift your focus to be more about spending time with him?

3. If you are struggling with spending consistent time with him, take a minute to examine your heart. Why is this so difficult? Take note of any idols you have made out of circumstances in your life. Bring them to God and ask for his forgiveness.

Discovering Grace
For
Your Race

Day Fifty

Apportioned Grace

"But to each one of us grace has been given as Christ apportioned it" Ephesians *4:7.*

Jesus gives gifts to all of us for the perfecting of the work of ministry. The grace that you are given is a gift to help you accomplish what you were called to do.

I had to find out the hard way that the amount of grace that was given to others was not the amount that was given to me. I spent years comparing and doubting myself because I was ignorant of this. The amount of grace given to raise my eight children was purposely allocated to me to save me from losing my mind and dignity. It is by God's grace that I am in my right mind to even write this devotional! Through His amazing grace, He has instilled patience, love, endurance and an enormous level of peace in me.

My house is always filled with screaming kids at all times of the day. This would drive most insane. To add to this, I have seven fluffy dogs that feel more like friends to me. Yet, they also require another level of grace. I know that this is unusual in most homes. But God always gives the right portion of grace to those that need it.

Your story or assignment may not include eight children. Maybe it's that one child with special needs or those three girls that only you can handle. It may be those stubborn boys who nobody understands but because of the grace on your life you are their perfect role model. The point is only you have the apportioned measure of grace for that specific assignment. I promise you the grace you were given was purposely apportioned to you so that you can succeed.

The next time you look at your situation and you think there is no way I can handle this, or your mind is contemplating that this is just too much for me, know that you have been given just the right amount of grace to finish your race.

Prayer: *Lord, you promised you would not put more on me then I can bear. I know that the measure of grace you have given me is sufficient for the task on hand. I will be humble and patient and will bear others in love. Thank you for your grace that has been given to me. Amen.*

Reflection Questions

1. Think about what you are responsible for, what has God called you to do that only you can do?

2. List a few things that you may need God to give you a little more grace for.

Finding Grace

"But he said to me, 'My grace is sufficient for you, for my power is made perfect in weakness.' Therefore, I will boast all the more gladly about my weaknesses, so that Christ's power may rest on me" 2 Corinthians 12:9.

It is mind boggling to me how the Scriptures let me know that my power is made perfect in weakness. Weakness has never made me feel at home. It's still a foreign concept I honestly dislike. When I'm vacationing in the land of the weak, I feel like I actually get weaker. Yet, I've learned emotions are actually as fickle as the weather. At least, the weather out here in New York City is fickle. One day it's 60 degrees the next day it's 11 degrees but feels like -12 degrees! It's been a humbling process to learn that our emotions are not reliable. We identify being weak with moments of weakness.

Raising eight children have afforded me many opportunities to train my children to be brave and strong. As I continue in this daily investment, I've realized that my early motherhood was missing a key ingredient: I had forgotten to teach my children the value of rest and the gift of help.

I shielded them from vulnerability. I didn't want them to see me distressed, battered or broken. I had to find the grace to be transparent about my life's reality, the truth about my life and the struggles it contained. For the sake of not wanting them to struggle or face the hard lessons of life, I failed to allow them to find the grace that will help them carry out their own life's mission.

In 2 Corinthians 12:9 God encourages us to boast about our weakness. It's almost like an oxymoron: ever thought about it like that? He's telling us His unmerited divine assistance is more than enough. It's an invitation to make our beds in a place of supernatural comfort, even while experiencing chaos breaking loose in our lives.

Nonetheless, I encourage you today to know God's grace is sufficient for every task you have been assigned to carry out. You were created for a purpose that only you can fulfill. Go forth and slay the day as you pray to find the grace that is set aside just for you.

Prayer: *Father, Today I purpose myself to find the grace I need to be all that I was created to be. I will trust that you have given me a measure of grace to carry out my assignment. I will go forth and do everything you have me to do. Amen.*

Reflection Questions

1. Are you able to identify your area of weakness?

2. Are you comfortable with getting real with yourself and facing the hard truth about areas where you are weak?

3. What are ways you can allow yourself to be more transparent when it come to you needing help?

Day Fifty-Two

Great Grace

"With great power the apostles continued to testify to the resurrection of the Lord Jesus. And God's grace was so powerfully at work in them all" Acts 4:33.

Imagine you are someone facing the pressure of having to go to a shelter with your five- year- old son, being told once again that you were not eligible for an apartment. Well a friend of mine experienced this very thing. Her mother would not take them in, nor any of her friends. On top of housing trouble, her son was having complications in school, being bullied, and wanting to harm himself. Having child services breathing down her neck, trying to take yet another child from her! Can you imagine this overwhelming pressure seizing you and all you had to hold on to is the strength that can only come from God's grace?

Months later, we connected, and she began to share with me her powerful testimony. It was a beautiful sunny afternoon as we sat on a rickety park bench in Harlem, this dear friend of mine with red almond shaped eyes and one tear of joy running down her cheek, began pouring out her grateful heart to me. She said she knew God sustained her through the tough times. He regulated her mind and kept her from losing her son. After four years of living from shelter to shelter and home to home, God opened a door that allowed her to move into a beautiful spacious apartment! Even though her son & her slept on the floor, for a short time, she watched God's supernatural provision provide not only furniture, but clothes for her ever- growing son! Not only clothes, but her and her son never went without food although she was unemployed. As she looked back it was God's grace that rested on her to make it through all that she did. Now with tears profusely running from my eyes, as I listened to her testimony, knowing that even when her back was up against the wall, God kept her through it all!

God's great grace brings supernatural power and provision. The Apostles were able to testify with power of Jesus' resurrection even through their trails. Grace is the catalyst to the supernatural where God has access to move through your life. All it takes is for you to say yes to activate God's grace within you that will enable you to move in divine authority. With this great grace, you are now equipped to walk, move and speak as God himself strengthens you. As you surrender to your heavenly father, you now transition from your own natural ability, to God's supernatural power.

Whether you are working two jobs while balancing school, or you are barely making ends meet financially, you can quiet your worrisome thoughts and rest in Jesus. Being encouraged that you have an eternal, magnanimous power working within you, and you can rest assure that this virtue will not fail you!

Prayer: *Father, I know that you understand every one of my weaknesses. I ask for your divine grace to empower me to accomplish that which I cannot do by my own strength. For through Jesus we can do all things. I repent for any disbelief that I've harbored in my heart. .I come into agreement with your word that all things are possible to those that believe! Father, I lean on your strength, and I put my trust in you that all things are working together for my good! Thank you, God for your great grace, in Jesus name. Amen.*

Reflection Questions

1. Do you recognize at least three things that you are grateful for daily?

2. How can you be more encouraging to others who are going through a hard time?

3. Like our physical bodies, our faith needs to be exercised daily. How can you exercise your faith today?

Restores Grace

"And the God of all grace, who called you to his eternal glory in Christ, after you have suffered a little while, will himself restore you and make you strong, firm and steadfast" 1 Peter 5:10.

Have you ever experienced frustration to the point where you wanted to cut all ties and give up?

Every morning as my feet would grace the ground my heart would plummet with a heavy weight of depression and doubt. I can recall talking to God as I would begin my day asking him, "why?" Why was I suffering, with no end in sight? I continued to go to Church, Homeschool my children and mask my pain with a smile. All around me it seemed like God was stripping me of everything I loved.

Scripture says, "Hope deferred make the heart sick," but at this point I felt as if my heart became shriveled up like a prune and all the love was eternally drained out of it. I realized God was doing something in me. He was making me aware of how much I needed Him. I started to pray more, and I realized the more I prayed the more He began to restore me. He showed me that the more I trusted in His power, the more He gave me restoration. I didn't realize through my dark times, God was teaching me to be a light for others. He taught me how to redeem the remnants and help others in my same situation.

This may be you in this very moment. You may feel like the more you try, the harder things get, but I'm here to tell you that God has a greater plan and purpose. All you must do is trust in Him and He will work in his majestic ways.

Prayer: *Lord God, we thank you for teaching us how to get past all things that we are facing. We bless you for giving us grace for our race and ask you to keep guiding us in our walk through you. We love you father and bless your name. Amen.*

Reflection Questions

1. Have you found that place where you position yourself to pray in your home?

2. What are some scriptures you can memorize to remind you of God's grace when you are frustrated?

3. Sometimes the best way to cheer up is to do something nice for others. What small gesture can you do for someone when you are feeling down?

Uncover

Keys to Success

Committed to Success

"Commit to the LORD whatever you do, and he will establish your plans"- Proverbs 16:3.

S uccess defines the accomplishment of an aim or purpose. The name Victoria comes from Latin which means "victory." We attribute our success to degrees achieved, positions of high stature earned, or to our abilities and capabilities.

For years, our ancestors instilled in us that success is measured by our acts and what we can do for ourselves and how well we do it, rather than us entrusting every plan unto God. The keyword here is trust. Trusting is not easy, especially when we've been conditioned to be independent and strong- willed. As a woman, you have no time to wait around for things to get done. You have to make it happen and set the order. After all, the household depends on us. The Lord is our Father, yet His dealing with His children can be slightly different.

He knows we are capable of getting it done. Yet, all he requires is for us to basically entrust Him with all of it as he establishes our plans. Do me a favor, just take a second and breathe. You are exactly where you need to be. This book is confirmation that it is now your time. Be proud of yourself as you walk in the success of your self-growth.

Prayer: Father, Today I commit every plan in my heart and mind over to you. You have given me a hope and a future. Lead me into your purpose for my life. My life is in your hands.

Amen.

Reflection Questions

1. How can you demonstrate your trust for God today?

2. Is there anyone that can keep you accountable on your path to success?

3. Are you feeling confident in yourself? If not, remember that God calls you qualified despite the expectations of other people.

Success Is in Our Obedience

"Work willingly at whatever you do, as though you were working for the Lord rather than for people"- Colossians 3:23 (NLT).

Last year, God placed upon my heart the desire to launch a new women's' ministry in my church. I decided to kick it off with a women's retreat. But as I prayed about what the theme would be, God fell silent. After almost a year of silence, God finally spoke. Elated with the new ministry God had given me, I set to work and soon all of the details fell into place. But when it came time for women to sign up for the retreat, few women came forward. Week after week I checked the empty sign- up sheet, hoping someone might change her mind and attend. When it came time to decide if I should cancel the retreat, the doubts of my adequacy came to the forefront of my mind. Like Hester Prynne in *The Scarlett Letter*, I felt like I was wearing a four- letter F across my chest in blazing red ink for all to see: Fail.

Analyzing Jesus' three- year ministry on earth by human standards, he suffered the biggest ministry failure of them all. Sure, in the beginning, it was waving palm branches and thousands of adoring fans. But once he started preaching the piercing truth of the gospel, only one disciple dared to come to His crucifixion. But Jesus never fed his ego with the adoration of others. He was secure in the approval of His father.

As Christians, we measure the success of our ministries by the numbers of people who sit in the pews hanging on our every word. We compare our numbers to other ministries in our own church as well as other churches and think because we don't yield the same amount of interested members as other ministries, we must be failures. Yet, Jesus measures our success by our *obedience*, not *attendance*.

When we seek to change one person's life with the gospel, He replaces our four- letter word with another one:

Free.

Prayer: *May we measure our success by our obedience, not by others' attendance. Amen.*

Discussion Questions

1. Why is it so easy to measure our value by our attendance rather than our attendance?

2. Why do you think the world values what we can measure rather than our mere obedience to God's call?

3. How can you stop equating your value with what is measurable rather than obedience to God's call?

Getting Out of a Spiritual Rut

"Do not cling to events of the past or dwell on what happened long ago. Watch for the new thing I am going to do. It is happening already—you can see it now" Isaiah 43:18.

❝That's just who I am," my friend remarked after we had a conversation about how we wanted to grow spiritually in the next year. My friend, after feeling a bit pressured to take on a new spiritual discipline as a way to grow said, "Yeah, I'm just not good at that. That's just the way I am." It was shocking to hear her say that.

I know I have thought that myself before I knew the Lord. But now that I have walked with the Lord for over twenty years, I've come to understand that the Lord loves us too much to leave us the way we are. He wants to constantly be doing new things in my life. God wants us to conform to His image, but we have to do the work. Make a resolution to practice a spiritual discipline. Maybe you read the Word consistently, but have you taken an afternoon to worship and to get alone with God? Has God spoken to you and have you been obedient to what he has said? Do you journal the revelations that you discover in the bible?

Along with a new spiritual discipline, do you have an accountability group or person that you can go to when you need wise counsel or having trouble overcoming a sin? Prayerfully consider whom God might have placed in your path to help you in your spiritual journey. Although it is tempting, we are not made to walk through life alone. God has placed us in community with others to sharpen one another and to help each other become more like Christ. Some people have been walking longer in their walks than others and therefore have wisdom to share. Ask someone who you think is spiritually older than you.

They may help you avoid the pitfalls of spiritual life and can spare you precious time and energy making the same mistakes.

Finally, you can avoid getting stuck in a spiritual rut by attending church regularly. Becoming connected in a church body helps meet your needs for connection and community.

Instead of sitting alone night after night, wouldn't it be great to invite church friends over for food, games and fun? Not only can you enjoy deep, meaningful relationships but also have some fun in the process.

Perhaps that sounds intimidating to you, but a deeper walk with God is possible. You just have to think outside the box and faithfully pursue something new. The Lord will honor it.

Prayer: *Lord, help me to be aware of the new things you are doing in my life.*

Reflection Questions

1. Why is it easier to dwell in the past rather than looking forward to the future?

2. When you feel dry spiritually, what new ways do you practice connecting with God?

3. Which of the three ways mentioned above do you have trouble with the most? In what way do you think God is calling you to practice it in a new way?

I'm Possible

"Enlarge the place of your tent, stretch your tent curtains wide, do not hold back; lengthen your cords, strengthen your stakes" -Isaiah 54:2.

I had to stretch my tent stakes when I started my first business. There were times when I thought my tent was going to fall completely and utterly apart. But God requires us to have faith and not hold back. Here I was starting a business with no savings, no mentor, no schooling and no business experience. Yet He was pressing me to start a company with faith.

There were many things I had to do in order to realize the dream God had waiting for me. I had to take chances and prepare my family. The stretch was real. I had to make sacrifice on top of sacrifice. Not only me but my family too. They too were the proud partners of "Joyful Party's Boutique." I didn't hold back and because I chose to dream, big JPB flourished. My company ended up being hired at the Barclays Center, The Armory, and even the Rockefeller Center and many other large arenas.

Think about something you thought you couldn't possibly do. That thing that would totally stretch you beyond your comfort zone. Prepare yourself for it then go for it. It will work out. For it isn't impossible but tell yourself I'm-possible.

Prayer: *Abba, help me to walk by faith and not by sight. Stretch me father, help me do things I thought were impossible. Help me understand that if I take a leap of faith and prepare myself for what you promised I will succeed in all things that I can possibly dream for.*

Reflection Questions

1. How can you enlarge your dreams? Remember God doesn't want us to hold back.

2. Have you prayed to God about your dreams and goals? Are they in the will of God?

3. What is something you can do today that you wouldn't do usually?

Make It Sweet

"For I know the plans I have for you declares the LORD, 'plans to prosper you and not harm you, plans to give you hope and a future"- Jeremiah 29:11.

Many times, when we seem to have not found our unique purpose in life, we catch ourselves feeling like we may never prosper or that there is no hope or future for us. But this scripture tells us otherwise. Let me remind you that your plans may not be God's plans. But at the end of the day, He wants to prosper you and give you hope and a future.

God has this amazing way of telling us to write the vision and make it plain. But when we do, it seems that He laughs at it, tears it up, and begins to rewrite the plans He had for us before we were formed in our mother's womb. There were countless times I wrote down what I thought was best for my family. Yet, God had other plans and I am so grateful. It's not that He didn't want me to dream big, because I did. But He needed me to trust Him. It's impossible to please God without faith. It's even more heart wrenching to God when you put your plans before His plans for your life.

There's a greater future for you. You must dream big but at the end of the dream, allow God to rewrite it to make it sweet.

Prayer: *Heavenly Father, we thank you that your plans are above our own and that you teach us how to follow you dutifully. We appreciate the sweetness of your plans and ask you to keep teaching us more. We long to be more like you and to dream bigger than ever. Father keep our dreams great and help us go further than before as we let go and let you have your way. Amen.*

Reflection Questions

1. Have you fully accepted God's plan for your life?

2. Are you acting in the instructions that God has given you?

3. Do you truly believe that God has plans to prosper you?

Level Up!

"But seek first his kingdom and his righteousness, and all these things will be given to you as well"- Matthew 6:33.

Now that you are fully aware of who you are and have an idea on what it means to dream big by now, you should now that it would be impossible for you to be selfish in those dreams because you are led by the spirit. In fact, the Holy Spirit does a great job of expanding those dreams as you grow from level to level. This means you must let yourself rise above limitations and strive to do bigger things knowing that, that ever- present help in time of need is right by your side to guide you through.

I can recall being in my early 20's pursuing a career in the music industry. I was in a group called "Uzziah" with two other talented vocalists. You may recognize this name Uzziah from the Bible, it means "child of the Lord and strength". Now, I didn't know this at the time, but I named the group and was not seeking righteousness at the time. I didn't know though that God had a meticulous plan. We never made it to the Grammy's or the B.E.T awards. We actually broke up two years after starting. It was then when my journey for righteousness began. It's only when I began to seek first the kingdom of God that all these other things began to be added to my life. A year later, I got married to an amazing man of God and my journey into all the things God wanted for me came to be.

Never allow anyone to discourage you from your dreams or make you feel less than because you haven't yet made it to where you want to be. God requires us to level up to his plans, but we must first seek his kingdom and his righteousness. Ask yourself this question today, "Am I leveling up to what God wants me to be?" After you've really looked into yourself let's pray.

Prayer: *Jesus, I trust in your strength to make all my dreams come true and that all my dreams will level up to yours.*

Reflection Questions

1. Are you growing from your mistakes? Are you making attempts to turn away from your sin?

2. Do you listen to what others have to say about you? Remind yourself that you are precious in God's eyes.

3. What is one thing you can level up in today?

40017396R10077

Made in the USA
Middletown, DE
22 March 2019